rSkills® Tests
Progress Monitoring and Summative Assessments for Whole- and Small-Group Instruction

ISBN-13: 978-0-545-07667-8
ISBN-10: 0-545-07667-6

2 3 4 5 6 7 8 9 10   31   17 16 15 14 13 12 11 10 09

Contents

Contents *(continued)*

READ 180 Overview

READ 180 is an intensive reading intervention program designed to support students whose reading achievement is below grade level. The program directly addresses individual needs through adaptive and instructional software, high-interest reading material and literature, and direct instruction in reading and writing skills.

Assessment in *READ 180*

READ 180 has a comprehensive assessment system to ensure that students are progressing toward grade level. These assessments can help you place students in the program, plan classroom instruction, and monitor your students' reading progress throughout the year. The table below provides an overview of the assessments included as part of the *READ 180* program.

Assessment	Purpose
Scholastic Reading Inventory™	• To determine the appropriate instructional level for each student. • To monitor progress.
READ 180 Software	• To assess comprehension skills, vocabulary acquisition, word recognition, fluency, and spelling/encoding. • To group and regroup students for targeted instruction.
READ 180 rSkills® Tests	• To monitor progress with *rBook®* skills taught in group instruction. • To provide summative assessments at midyear and end-of-year.
Reading Counts! Quizzes	• To assess independent reading progress.

This book contains *READ 180 rSkills Tests* to use with your students. You can find more information about other assessment components in the *READ 180 Placement, Assessment, and Reporting Guide.*

Curriculum-Based Assessment

Curriculum-based assessment occurs in the context of learning and instruction. *READ 180* curriculum-based assessment consists of periodic classroom-based tests that are aligned with *READ 180 rBook* curriculum and instruction. These tests are criterion-referenced to lessons and ask students to demonstrate mastery of specific skills they were taught, rather than assessing more general achievement or reading proficiency.

READ 180's curriculum-based assessment can help you to:

- Measure students' reading success within *READ 180*.
- Monitor students at the end of workshop lessons.
- Provide information on instructional effectiveness.
- Reteach and reinforce using *Resources for Differentiated Instruction*.

About *READ 180 rSkills Tests*

READ 180 rSkills Tests are curriculum-based assessments that are aligned to the *READ 180 rBook* and *Teacher's Edition.* Each test assesses students' ability to demonstrate understanding of specific reading skills. The tests are designed to monitor content progress and support instruction, and are aligned to core Reading and Language Arts contents standards.

Purpose of *rSkills Tests*

The *READ 180 rSkills Tests* enable you to assess students' transfer of specific reading skills taught in each *rBook* Workshop. The tests are designed to be used flexibly to meet assessment, grading, and reporting needs.

You can use the *rSkills Tests* to do one or more of the following:

- Track students' *rBook* skills progress throughout the year.
- Target specific skills for individual and group-differentiated instruction.
- Expose students to material they will encounter in grade-level text and on high-stakes tests.

Testing at Grade Level

The *rSkills Tests* accommodate students at their reading level as well as moving them toward grade-level text. There are two forms of each test—one with below grade-level comprehension passages (Level a) and one with grade-level passages (Level b). Passage readability was determined using multiple measures, including the Lexile Framework®, which matches students to text at the appropriate reading level.

Test Levels a and b assess the *same skills* and have the *same item format.* However, as the table below shows, the two levels differ in Lexile® range, passage length, and question structure.

Leveling Criteria	Below Grade-Level Tests Level a	Grade-Level Tests Level b
Lexile range	250–599 L	600–950 L
Length	150–200 words	200–600 words
Structure	Shorter, simpler sentences	Longer, more complex sentences

You will find below grade-level tests (Level a) for progress monitoring on pages 39–112. Grade-level tests (Level b) begin on page 113. Summative assessments for below grade-level (Level a) begin on page 193 and grade-level (Level b) on page 239.

Supporting Your Classroom Instruction With *rSkills Tests*

The *rSkills Tests* are designed to be administered throughout the school year, as you use the *READ 180 rBook* curriculum and *Teacher's Edition.* There are *five tests* for progress monitoring at each level (below grade-level and grade-level). Each test assesses specific skills taught in consecutive Workshops—as well as retesting skills from previous Workshops.

Test Selection	Number of Test Items
Comprehension	10 (passage-based multiple choice)
Vocabulary, Word Study and Morphology	10
Grammar, Usage, and Mechanics	10
Open Response	2 (constructed response)
Writing	1 writing prompt

Administering the tests after the second, fourth, sixth, eighth, and ninth Workshops will enable you to assess your students' ability to apply the skills taught during instruction.

The *rSkills* summative assessments for Levels a and b test the same skills with 40 multiple-choice test items and a writing prompt. In addition, the Midyear and End-of-Year Tests have an optional 10-item Listening subtest at the end of each test.

The *rSkills* Summative Midyear Test for each level is intended to be administered after Workshop 5. The End-of-Year Test is intended to be administered after Workshop 9.

The *rSkills Tests* correlate with the *READ 180 rBook* in a number of ways, allowing your students to transfer and apply targeted Workshop skills and vocabulary.

rBook and *rSkills Test* Alignment	How This Helps *READ 180* Students
All skills are tested using language similar to the way they are taught in the *rBook.*	Students can transfer and apply what they have learned.
rSkills Test passages include fiction and nonfiction text.	Students can practice applying comprehension skills with a variety of reading selections in the *rBook* and *rSkills Tests.*
rSkills Test passages assume some background knowledge and vocabulary from the *rBook* Workshops.	Students can focus on applying skills, rather than having to master unfamiliar concepts.
Skills are taught and tested recursively throughout the *rBook* and *rSkills Tests.*	Students master skills over time and throughout the program.
Graphical text elements (e.g., charts) are part of each *rBook* Workshop and each *rSkills Test.*	Students can read and understand information and reference material that they encounter in most of their content-area textbooks and on tests.

Background on *rSkills Test* Development

READ 180 rSkills Tests were developed to reflect the *rBook* curriculum and support progress monitoring and summative assessment in Whole- and Small-Group Instruction. In consultation with key assessment experts, development of the *rSkills Tests* consisted of the following four major steps:

1. Reviewing the *READ 180 rBook* curriculum, core standards, and state standard frameworks to identify key reading skills to assess.

2. Creating item-writing specifications and sample item formats, and determining item skill distribution across all tests based on the *READ 180 rBook* curriculum.

3. Writing items and comprehension passages according to specifications and analysis of skills and item formats included on state standardized tests.

4. Reviewing items for content validity.

Content Review Process

Curriculum-based assessments such as the *rSkills Tests* typically do not undergo the depth of empirical review used when developing standardized tests. However, it is important to construct these assessments with the same care and adherence to curricular goals. This process involves content review by a panel of assessment and reading experts to ensure test quality.

Establishing Test Validity

The *rSkills Tests* were rigorously reviewed to ensure that they are appropriate and fair. Five educators examined each item and test for content validity to make sure that it:

- Reflects *READ 180* assessment goals.

- Matches the scope and sequence of skills taught in the *READ 180 rBook.*

- Aligns with the explicit instruction in the *rBook* and *Teacher's Edition.*

- Is fair, and does not favor or penalize any group of students based on their personal background.

Item Review Process

The *rSkills Test* content reviewers were trained in the review methodology and received materials to support the review process. These materials included the overall assessment goals, review criteria, and sample *rBook* instructional material.

The reviewers assessed each test as a whole, as well as focusing on individual test items. Any disputed items were replaced. Replacement items then underwent a second round of content review.

Test Review Criteria The reviewers examined each test for item group bias to ensure that the collective group of items does not offend or unfairly penalize or privilege any group of students based on their race, gender, or ethnicity.

Item Review Criteria The reviewers assessed each test question according to the criteria shown in the table below.

Review Criterion	Description
Content Validity	Does the item appropriately assess the intended skill?
Contribution to a Mastery/ Non-Mastery Inference	Will a student's response to this item contribute to an accurate inference about the student's mastery of the intended skill the item measures?
Instructional Sensitivity	Does it appear that students who are taught the skill through the *rBook* instruction will demonstrate a change in performance as measured by the item?
Bias	Might this item offend or unfairly penalize any group of students on the basis of personal characteristics such as race, gender, or ethnicity?

Using the *rSkills Tests*

READ 180 rSkills Tests are available in print and interactive formats. This book contains reproducible pages that you can photocopy and distribute to students.

When Do I Administer a Test?

The *rSkills Tests* are designed to be administered approximately every six weeks for progress monitoring, depending on your instructional pacing using the *READ 180 rBook*. The table below shows suggested administration.

rSkills Test	ADMINISTER AFTER COMPLETING . . .
TEST 1	Workshops 1 (Fires Out of Control) and 2 (Coming to America)
TEST 2	Workshops 3 (Bud, Not Buddy) and 4 (Bullies Beware)
MIDYEAR TEST	Workshop 5
TEST 3	Workshops 5 (Secrets of the Mummy's Tomb) and 6 (Good Sports)
TEST 4	Workshops 7 (Taming Wild Beasts) and 8 (Food: The Good, the Bad, and the Gross)
TEST 5	Workshop 9 (No Small Hero)
END-OF-YEAR TEST	Workshop 9

Which Test Level Do I Assign?

The test level you use will depend on your assessment purpose and each student's reading level. Initially, we recommend using below grade-level tests (Level a) for all students.

Below Grade-Level Tests (Level a) Use these tests for significantly struggling readers, English-language learners, or students in *READ 180* Levels 1 and 2. If a student scores consistently well, you might discuss trying a grade-level test later in the year. Be sure to prepare the student for the change in test difficulty and allow additional testing time.

Grade-Level Tests (Level b) Use these tests for students reading at or near grade level. Passages in these tests are longer than those in Level a. Item formats are similar to those on high-stakes tests. You can use Level b tests to see how your students are performing against grade-level standards or more informally for exposing students to the kinds of standardized tests they will take.

How Do I Use the Open-Response and Writing Questions?

Each of the *rSkills Tests 1–5* has two optional open-response questions designed to elicit short constructed responses. These questions test literal and inferential comprehension of the test passages. You can include these questions as part of the formal test or use them for review, or for a quick writing-on-demand opportunity.

Each *rSkills Test* also has a writing prompt. These prompts assess the kinds of writing students have learned and practiced in the *rBook* Workshops. You can include these prompts as part of the formal test or use them for review and writing practice.

Scope and Sequence of Tested Skills

The table below shows the skills that are assessed on each of the *rSkills Tests 1–5.* This scope and sequence applies to below grade-level (Level a) and grade-level (Level b) tests.

	Comprehension*	Vocabulary/Word Study	Grammar, Usage, and Mechanics	Writing
TEST 1	• Main Idea and Details • Sequence of Events	• Prefixes • Suffixes • Synonyms • Antonyms	• Identifying Sentences and Fragments • Correcting Sentence Fragments • Using End Punctuation • Using Capitals • Identifying Simple and Compound Sentences	Expository
TEST 2	• Main Idea and Details • Sequence of Events • Character • Setting • Plot • Summarize	• Word Families • Compound Words • Context Clues • Homophones	• Correcting Run-On Sentences • Using Correct Verb Tense • Using Correct Word Order • Using Commas in a Series • Combining Sentences	Literary Response
TEST 3	• Character • Setting • Plot • Theme • Summarize • Problem and Solution	• Word Families • Homophones • Multiple-Meaning Words • Idioms	• Using Irregular Verbs • Subject-Verb Agreement • Using Commas With Introductory Words • Using Possessives • Using Conjunctions	Persuasive
TEST 4	• Summarize • Problem and Solution • Cause and Effect • Compare and Contrast	• Verb Endings • Suffixes • Using a Dictionary • Synonyms • Multiple-Meaning Words	• Using Subject and Object Pronouns • Using Adjectives That Compare • Avoiding Double Negatives • Using Quotation Marks • Using Compound Sentences	Descriptive
TEST 5	• Character • Setting • Plot • Theme • Cause and Effect • Compare and Contrast • Make Inferences	• Antonyms • Multiple-Meaning Words • Noun Endings • Using a Dictionary	• Identifying Sentences and Fragments • Correcting Sentence Fragments • Using Adverbs • Identifying Simple and Compound Sentences • Combining Sentences	Personal Narrative

*One comprehension question in each test relates to a graphic element (e.g., chart or table).

These same skills are assessed on the Midyear and End-of-Year Tests (Levels a and b). Midyear Tests assess skills drawn from Workshops 1–5. End-of-Year Tests assess skills drawn from all of the Workshops, 1–9. In addition, each Midyear and End-of-Year Test includes an optional Listening subtest that tests comprehension skills. The skills assessed in both of these tests are listed below.

	Comprehension*	Vocabulary/ Word Study	Grammar, Usage, and Mechanics	Writing	Listening
MIDYEAR TEST	• Sequence of Events • Plot, Setting, Character • Problem and Solution • Main Idea and Details • Summarize	• Prefixes • Suffixes • Synonyms • Antonyms • Homophones • Word Families • Context Clues • Compound Words • Idioms	• Identifying Sentences and Fragments • Correcting Sentence Fragments • Correcting Run-On Sentences • Using Capitals • Using Irregular Verbs • Using Conjunctions • Using Commas With Introductory Words • Using Correct Verb Tense • Using Correct Word Order • Using End Punctuation • Using Compound Sentences • Using Commas in a Series • Combining Sentences	• Expository	• Sequence of Events • Plot, Setting, Character • Problem and Solution • Main Idea and Details • Summarize
END-OF-YEAR TEST	• Sequence of Events • Plot, Setting, Character, Theme • Problem and Solution • Main Idea and Details • Summarize • Cause and Effect • Make Inferences • Compare and Contrast	• Verb Endings • Suffixes • Synonyms • Antonyms • Multiple-Meaning Words • Word Families • Context Clues • Homophones • Using A Dictionary • Latin and Greek Roots • Noun Endings	• Identifying Sentences and Fragments • Correcting Sentence Fragments • Using Subject and Object Pronouns • Using Adjectives That Compare • Avoiding Double Negatives • Using Possessives • Using Adverbs • Using Quotation Marks • Identifying Simple and Compound Sentences • Using Conjunctions • Combining Sentences	• Personal Narrative	• Sequence of Events • Make Inferences • Plot, Setting, Character • Problem and Solution • Main Idea and Details • Cause and Effect • Compare and Contrast • Summarize

*One comprehension question in each test relates to a graphic element (e.g., chart or table).

Preparing Students for an *rSkills Test*

READ 180 students may not have had successful test-taking experiences in the past. Many lack the skills and self-esteem needed to be successful on tests. However, you can help your students succeed on the *rSkills Tests* by creating a supportive testing environment.

Before administering the first *rSkills Test*, be sure to review appropriate test-taking strategies. These include careful reading, looking at all answers before making a choice, and pausing between selections. You may also wish to practice reading text passages as a class and modeling how to arrive at an answer.

Test-Taking Strategies

Following are specific strategies you can share with your students.

- **Review Workshop Skills** Revisit the opening or closing pages of the appropriate *rBook* Workshops to review the key Comprehension; Vocabulary/Word Study; Grammar, Usage, and Mechanics; and Writing skills that will be tested on the next *rSkills Test*.

- **Look for Important Ideas** When you read a comprehension passage, look for ideas you think might be important. Look especially at the first and last sentences in each paragraph. Take mental notes as you read.

- **Complete the Sentence** When you think you've got the right answer to a completion item or fill-in-the-blank question, read the sentence, inserting the answer you chose. Does it make sense? Does the answer match information from the passage?

- **Use Context Clues to Figure Out Unfamiliar Words** If you come across a vocabulary word you don't know, slow down and take some time to see if you can figure out what the word means. Look at the context clues before and after the word, as well as the surrounding sentences. Think about what the passage is saying. This can help you to determine the meaning of the word and to eliminate wrong answer choices.

- **Practice Time-Management Strategies** Use an *rSkills Test* to practice managing time effectively in test conditions. Review the total time allocated for a test and the amount of time you need to read the passages and answer each item. This will help you to determine how you should allocate your time.

- **Use Your Skips** If you are taking an *Interactive rSkills Test*, you can skip a question and return to answer it later. Skipping a question will not affect your results. Before you can submit a test and get a score, you will be reminded to answer any questions you skipped.

For more information, including lesson plans and activities, see the *READ 180 Test-Taking Strategies* book.

Using Print *rSkills* Tests

You can administer the print *rSkills Tests* during Whole- or Small-Group Instruction. If you are using Level b tests, students will require more time, since the passages on these tests are significantly longer. Students can mark or write their answers on the test pages or on a separate Test Answer Document. There is one Answer Document for the *rSkills Progress Monitoring Tests* and a different one for the *rSkills* Summative Midyear and End-of-Year Tests.

Preparing the Tests
Make copies of the appropriate reproducible test(s) included in this book and the Test Answer Document (pages 283–286). If you do not wish to use the open-response questions, simply omit that page when making copies.

Introducing the Tests
Explain to your students that they will be taking an *rSkills Test*. The test is divided into five sections (Comprehension; Vocabulary/Word Study; Grammar, Usage, and Mechanics; Open Response; and Writing). Each section contains questions based on skills they learned in the *rBook* Workshops. (The Midyear and End-of-Year Tests also have an optional subtest for Listening, which can be administered after the other subtests.)

Getting Started

1. Make sure each student has two sharpened pencils with erasers.
2. Distribute copies of the appropriate test (and the Test Answer Document).
3. Have students write their names and the date on the first test page or Test Answer Document. Have students write the test number on the Answer Document as well.
4. Read aloud the directions on the first page.
5. Tell students the amount of time you have planned for the test. This will vary, depending on which test level students are taking. You can allow students to take the tests at their own pace, depending on how you plan to use the assessment results.
6. Encourage students to read each multiple-choice question carefully and review the four answer choices before choosing an answer.
7. Remind students to write their open-response answers on the lines inside the answer boxes that are provided.
8. For the Writing prompt, students should write their responses on the test pages or on an Answer Document.

Answering the Sample Questions
For at least the first test, have your students answer the two sample questions. Review the answers (on the Test Answer Key) to make sure each student is comfortable with the test format and answer sheet procedure. Then have them turn the page to begin the test.

Using *Interactive rSkills Tests*

Students can take the *Interactive rSkills Tests* during their *READ 180* Software rotations. Students taking *Interactive rSkills Tests* will receive feedback on their correct and incorrect answers. *Interactive rSkills Tests* also offer automatic scoring and reporting. These features allow you to track individual student and group progress. The *Interactive rSkills Test* reports also enable you to target skills for individual and group-differentiated instruction (see page 17 for more information on reports).

If you are using the *Interactive rSkills Tests*, follow the step-by-step instructions in the *READ 180 Software Manual* to enroll your students and assign the tests through the *Scholastic Achievement Manager*™ (SAM). The *READ 180 Software Manual* also describes the students' computer test-taking experience. Reviewing this information will enable you to model for students how to take an *Interactive rSkills Test.*

Introducing the Tests

To take an *Interactive rSkills Test*, each student will need to log on to the *rSkills Test* software with a username and password. Encourage students to answer the on-screen sample questions. Check in with students after they have answered the sample questions to make sure they are comfortable using the software.

Scoring the Tests

The computer will automatically score your students' multiple-choice answers on the *Interactive rSkills Tests.* You can use SAM to score the open-response questions and the writing prompt using four- or six-point scoring rubrics.

Assigning Multiple Tests

Interactive rSkills Tests are available at two levels (Levels a and b), allowing you to use the tests for multiple purposes. You may choose to assign the below grade-level *Interactive rSkills Tests* (Level a) to assess your students' skills progress. However, at a later date you can also assign the grade-level tests (Level b) for follow-up assessment or for another reason.

Tips for Students

Share these tips with students before they take an *Interactive rSkills Test:*

1. Follow the prompts on each test screen.
2. Answer the sample questions before beginning a test.
3. You can skip a question and return to it later.
4. Use the scroll bar to view a complete comprehension passage.
5. If you run out of time, you can save a partially completed test.

rSkills Test Reports

When you use *Interactive rSkills Tests*, the *Scholastic Achievement Manager* (SAM) stores each student's test data. You can then view the data for individual students or groups of students through the *rSkills Test* reports.

The *rSkills Test* reports can help you to:

- Monitor your students' Comprehension; Vocabulary/Word Study; Grammar, Usage, and Mechanics; and Writing skills progress over time.
- Identify specific skills students are struggling with.
- Plan activities to target skills for Whole- and Small-Group Instruction.
- Review students' test answers and offer learning strategies for individual students.

The following table briefly describes the *rSkills Test* reports. You will find more detailed reports information in the *READ 180 Placement, Assessment, and Reporting Guide*.

Report Name	What It Shows
Student Skills Report	Individual student results of one *rSkills Test*
Student Progress Report	Individual student *rSkills Test* scores over time
Summary Skills Report	Aggregated *rSkills Test* results of one test for a class, group, or school
Summary Progress Report	Aggregated *rSkills Test* results over time for a class, group, or school
Student Test Printout	Individual student answers for one *rSkills Test*

Resources

When viewing *rSkills Test* reports on-screen, you will have access to a variety of skill-specific instructional resources through the *Scholastic Achievement Manager*. The *READ 180 Software Manual* contains detailed instructions on how to use this feature.

Scoring *rSkills Tests*

To score a print test, use the answer keys included in this book. The answer keys include sample answers for each open-response question to use as a guide when scoring your students' written answers. The computer will automatically score your students' multiple-choice answers on the *Interactive rSkills Tests.*

Using Scoring Guides

You can use the following four- or six-point rubrics to grade open-response questions—or create your own rubric.

4-Point Rubric

Score	Standard	Description
4 points	Exemplary	• Responds to the question. • Makes a statement, gives a description, paraphrases information, draws a conclusion, makes an inference or prediction, or offers an interpretation that is *well supported* by the text.
3 points	Proficient	• Responds to the question. • Makes a statement, gives a description, paraphrases information, draws a conclusion, makes an inference or prediction, or offers an interpretation that is *adequately supported* by the text.
2 points	Partially Sufficient	• Responds somewhat to the question. • Makes a statement, gives a description, paraphrases information, draws a conclusion, makes an inference or prediction, or offers an interpretation that is only *partially supported* by the text.
1 point	Insufficient	• Does not respond to the question. • Makes a statement, gives a description, paraphrases information, draws a conclusion, makes an inference or prediction, or offers an interpretation that is *unsupported* by the text.

6-Point Rubric

Score	Standard	Description
6 points	Exemplary	• Responds to the question. • Makes a statement, gives a description, paraphrases information, draws a conclusion, makes an inference or prediction, or offers an interpretation that is *well supported* by the text.
5 points	Proficient	• Responds to the question. • Makes a statement, gives a description, paraphrases information, draws a conclusion, makes an inference or prediction, or offers an interpretation that is *adequately supported* by the text.
4 points	Sufficient	• Responds to the question. • Makes a statement, gives a description, paraphrases information, draws a conclusion, makes an inference or prediction, or offers an interpretation that is *mostly supported* by the text.
3 points	Partially Sufficient	• Responds somewhat to the question. • Makes a statement, gives a description, paraphrases information, draws a conclusion, makes an inference or prediction, or offers an interpretation that is *partially supported* by the text.
2 points	Minimally Sufficient	• Responds minimally to the question. • Makes a statement, gives a description, paraphrases information, draws a conclusion, makes an inference or prediction, or offers an interpretation that is *minimally supported* by the text.
1 point	Insufficient	• Does not respond to the question. • Makes a statement, gives a description, paraphrases information, draws a conclusion, makes an inference or prediction, or offers an interpretation that is *unsupported* by the text.

Scoring Rubrics for Writing

You can use a 4-point or 6-point rubric to evaluate students' writing in response to the writing prompt on each rSkills Test—or you can create your own rubric.

The writing prompt in each test requires students to demonstrate a particular type of writing: expository, narrative, literary response, persuasive, or descriptive. To evaluate a student's writing, use the general Scoring Rubric (4-point or 6-point) below and the criteria for the specific type of writing (on the following pages) to help determine an overall score.

4-Point Rubric

Score	Standard	Description
4 points	Outstanding	The student's writing— • Clearly addresses the purpose of the writing task and meets all of the criteria for the type of writing. • Presents a central idea with relevant supporting facts, details, or examples. • Maintains a consistent point of view, focus, and organizational structure. • Uses varied sentence structures and excellent word choice. • Uses generally correct grammar, spelling, punctuation, and capitalization.
3 points	Good	The student's writing— • Addresses the purpose of the writing task and meets most of the criteria for the type of writing. • Presents a central idea with some supporting facts or details. • Maintains a mostly consistent point of view, focus, and organizational structure. • Uses some sentence variety and good word choice. • Has a few errors in grammar, spelling, punctuation, and capitalization, but these errors do not interfere with the reader's understanding of the writing.
2 points	Adequate	The student's writing— • Addresses part of the writing task and meets some criteria for the type of writing. • Suggests a central idea with limited supporting facts or details. • Maintains an inconsistent point of view, focus, and organizational structure. • Uses little sentence variety and ordinary word choice. • Has several errors in grammar, spelling, punctuation, and capitalization, and these errors may interfere with the reader's understanding of the writing.
1 point	Not proficient	The student's writing— • Shows little understanding of the writing task and does not meet the criteria for the type of writing. • Lacks a central idea but may include some facts or details. • Lacks a point of view, focus, and organizational structure. • Has no sentence variety and makes inaccurate word choices. • Has serious errors in grammar, spelling, punctuation, and capitalization, and these errors interfere with the reader's understanding of the writing.

6-point Scoring Rubric for Student Writing

Use the guidelines below to adapt the 4-point general scoring rubric for a 6-point proficiency scale.

Points	Level of Proficiency
6	Outstanding proficiency
5	Strong proficiency
4	Adequate proficiency
3	Limited proficiency
2	Low level of proficiency
1	Not proficient

Criteria for Specific Types of Writing

Expository Writing

- States a main topic or main idea
- Includes details to support or explain the topic or main idea
- Presents details in a logical order
- Uses linking words and transitions to connect details and ideas
- Summarizes or restates the topic at the end

Narrative Writing

- States and focuses on an event or main problem in the beginning
- Establishes a setting and introduces one or more characters
- Includes details that tell about the event, or plot events in which a character tries to solve the problem
- Presents details or events in a logical order, such as time order
- Uses linking words and transitions to connect details, events, and ideas
- Sums up the event and tells the writer's feelings about it, or presents a resolution of the main problem

Literary Response

- Identifies and states a main topic or main idea (i.e., the writer's connection to the story or piece of literature)
- Includes details to support or explain the topic or main idea
- Presents details in a logical order, such as time order
- Uses linking words and transitions to connect details and ideas
- Concludes the response with a summary of the story and/or the writer's feelings about it

Persuasive Writing

- States the writer's personal opinion or point of view
- Includes reasons or factual details to support the opinion or point of view
- Presents strong, convincing details in a logical order
- Uses linking words and transitions to connect details and ideas
- Summarizes or restates the writer's personal opinion or point of view at the end

Descriptive Writing

- States or identifies what is being described
- Includes descriptive details
- Presents interesting details in a logical order
- Uses linking words and transitions to connect details and ideas
- Sums up or restates the description and tells the writer's feelings about it

Using Scoring Charts

When scoring a print test, you may want to use a Scoring Chart to record and calculate student test scores. There is one Scoring Chart for *rSkills Tests 1–5* (Level a or b) and one for the Midyear and End-of-Year Tests (Level a or b).

To use a Scoring Chart, make a copy of the appropriate chart (on pages 22–23) for each student. For multiple-choice items, mark each correct answer by circling the item number. Mark each incorrect answer by crossing out the item number. To find the score for each subtest or the total test, count the number of items answered correctly. To find a percent score, divide the number of correct items by the total number of items and multiply by 100. For example, a student who answers 7 of 10 items correctly has a score of 7/10: $7 \div 10 = 0.7 \times 100 = 70\%$.

For Open Response questions (in Tests 1–5), mark the number of points earned by each response (on a 4-point or 6-point rubric).

For Writing prompts, mark the number of points for the student's writing (on a 4-point or 6-point rubric).

In the Midyear and End-of-Year Tests, the Listening subtest is optional and should be scored separately on the Scoring Chart.

Scoring Chart

for *rSkills*® Progress Monitoring Tests 1–5

Name _____   Date _____

Test _____   Level (a/b)* _____

SCORES					TEST SCORES	
Subtest					No. Correct/ Total	% Score
Comprehension						
1	2	3	4	5		
6	7	8	9	10	10	
Vocabulary/Word Study						
11	12	13	14	15		
16	17	18	19	20	10	
Grammar, Usage, and Mechanics						
21	22	23	24	25		
26	27	28	29	30	10	
Total Test (multiple-choice)					30	
Open Response (4-point or 6-point rubric)					Score (points)	
31						
32						
Writing (4-point or 6-point rubric)						

*a = Below grade-level, b = Grade-level

Scoring Chart

for *rSkills*® Summative Midyear and End-of-Year Tests

Name _____   Date _____

Test _____   Level (a/b)* _____

SCORES					TEST SCORES	
Subtest					**No. Correct/ Total**	**% Score**
Comprehension						
1	2	3	4	5		
6	7	8	9	10		
11	12	13	14	15		
16	17	18	19	20		20	
Vocabulary/Word Study						
21	22	23	24	25		
26	27	28	29	30		10	
Grammar, Usage, and Mechanics						
31	32	33	34	35		
36	37	38	39	40		10	
Total Test (multiple-choice)						40	
Writing (4-point or 6-point rubric)					Score (points)	
Listening (optional)					**No. Correct/ Total**	**% Score**
41	42	43	44	45		
46	47	48	49	50		10	

*a = Below grade-level, b = Grade-level

Using *rSkills Test* Results

The *rSkills Tests* are designed to be used flexibly. You can use the results to meet a range of assessment, grading, and reporting needs. For example, you can use your students' *rSkills Test* results to plan individual and Small-Group Instruction to target specific skills. You will find skill-specific lessons and activities in *Resources for Differentiated Instruction* in your Teacher Bookshelf. You can also access downloadable resources through the *Scholastic Achievement Manager* (SAM).

Track Your Students' Progress

You can track skills progress for individual students using the Student *rSkills Test* Progress Chart on page 26. You may wish to file your students' scoring charts, progress charts, and copies of their tests in individual folders for conferencing and grading purposes. If you are using the *Interactive rSkills Tests,* use the reports to monitor and track individual, group, and class progress.

Target Specific Skills

For *rSkills Tests 1–5,* results provide useful information about your students' level of understanding for each tested skill. You may want to work individually with a student to review his or her skill weaknesses as shown on an *rSkills Test.* Use the *READ 180 rBook* to return to the appropriate workshop and revisit readings and responses.

If multiple students had difficulty with a particular skill on an *rSkills Test,* group those students to reteach the skill using *Resources for Differentiated Instruction.*

Provide Grade-Level Material

If your students are mastering skills on the Level a *rSkills Tests,* consider administering a Level b test at the next testing period, following completion of two *READ 180 rBook* Workshops. The Level b tests follow the same format but use longer, more difficult passages and more complex item structure.

Summative Assessments

You can use students' test results on the Midyear and End-of-Year Tests for summative assessments—to determine students' mastery of the content and skills taught during the first half of the year or the entire year. You may also use summative test results to help determine student grades.

Reviewing Results With Students

After each *rSkills Test,* you may wish to meet with groups of students or one-on-one to discuss test results. You can review the test answers using the completed test or Test Answer Document. For *Interactive rSkills Tests*, use the Student Test Printout Report. Remember also to grade the open-response and writing questions using the *Scholastic Achievement Manager* (SAM). When reviewing an *rSkills Test*, you may wish to try the following strategies to help students understand their results and build confidence for future tests.

Discussing Progress

- Share the overall score with a student before discussing strengths and weaknesses. Have students record the score in the Student Log in their *READ 180 rBooks*.
- Ensure that students know which questions (and skills) they got correct and those that require more practice.
- Check the test level. If students struggled with a Level b test, remind them that it contains difficult text and explain why you gave them the test at this level.
- Review students' previous *rSkills Test* results and discuss or preview the requirements (and level) of their next test.

Revisiting the Test

- Identify and explain how to recognize the skill for each question.
- Encourage the student to read the question and answer choices aloud.
- Analyze each incorrect answer and encourage the student to "think aloud" about how he or she arrived at that choice.
- Have the student explain why an answer is correct or incorrect.

Reteaching Strategies

- Briefly review the skill (e.g., how to find the main idea in a passage).
- Use the *rBook* to revisit how a skill was described where students first encountered it, and provide some meaningful examples.
- For comprehension questions, use a question the student answered correctly to model how an answer is supported by the passage.

Sharing Results With Parents

You may wish to share an individual student's test results with parents or caregivers. You can do this by sending a letter home or at a parent-teacher conference. You will find a sample Parent Letter on page 27.

Student *rSkills*® Test Progress Chart

Name _____

TEST	LEVEL (a/b)*	TEST DATE	TEST SCORE		Comprehension	Vocabulary/ Word Study	Grammar, Usage, and Mechanics	Open Response (Rubric)		Writing
			NO. CORRECT	% SCORE	NO. CORRECT	NO. CORRECT	NO. CORRECT	QUESTION 1	QUESTION 2	PROMPT
TEST 1			30		10	10	10			
TEST 2			30		10	10	10			
MIDYEAR			40		20	10	10	Listening 10	%	
TEST 3			30		10	10	10			
TEST 4			30		10	10	10			
TEST 5			30		10	10	10			
END-OF-YEAR			40		20	10	10	Listening 10	%	

Notes

*a = Below grade-level, b = Grade-level

Parent Letter

Date _____

Dear Parent or Guardian,

_____ is enrolled in *READ 180*®, an intensive reading improvement program. As a student in this program, _____ receives instruction on key Comprehension; Vocabulary/Word Study; Grammar; and Writing skills. About every six to eight weeks,_____ takes a *READ 180 rSkills*® *Progress Monitoring Test*. These tests enable him/her to practice and apply the reading and writing skills learned in class.

Here are _____'s latest *rSkills Test* results:

Test Date _____

Test Result _____ /30 _____

Test Score _____ % _____

Comprehension	Vocabulary/ Word Study	Grammar, Usage, and Mechanics	Open Response
/10	/10	/10	___ out of ___

Here are some things you can do at home to help support your child's reading and writing progress:

- Make reading a daily activity by reading with your child for 20 minutes every day.
- Encourage your child to write letters, postcards, or emails.
- Consider sharing with your child the types of things you are reading. For example, talk about a magazine article that you read.

Thank you for taking the time to help improve _____'s reading skills. If I can be of any assistance, or if you have questions, please feel free to contact me.

Sincerely,

Administering the Listening Tests

In the rSkills summative assessments, each Midyear and End-of-Year Test (for Levels a and b) has a Listening subtest. This is an optional subtest provided for teachers who may want to assess their students' listening comprehension skills.

The Listening subtest uses standard listening passages and testing formats that you might see on statewide assessments in some states and on tests for English language learners (ELL). In *READ 180*, these subtests can be used to:

- help assess students' English language development through a listening format (in addition to the reading, writing, and speaking commonly used in the classroom);
- assess students' abilities to apply comprehension skills in a different medium (other than print);
- help students become familiar with the Listening tests they will take during statewide assessments or national standardized tests.

Use the following information and directions to administer the Listening subtests.

Description of the Listening Tests

In each Midyear and End-of-Year Test, there is a 2-page Listening subtest at the end of the test. The Listening subtest consists of two passages (one fiction and one nonfiction) and ten multiple-choice questions. There are five questions for each passage, based on the comprehension skills taught in *READ 180*.

When administering a Listening subtest, the teacher reads each passage aloud. After each passage, the teacher reads five questions, one at a time. Students listen to the passage and to each question. In response, students choose the best answer to each question.

The passages and questions appear only in the teacher directions for administering the Listening subtests (pages 29–36); they do not appear on the student pages. The answer choices for each question appear in the student test. Students read the answer choices independently and choose the best answer to each question. (Note: If you feel that your students will need help in reading the answer choices, you may read them aloud. To do so, you will need to refer to the student pages for the Listening subtest.)

In the following directions, you will find the reading passages and questions to be read aloud for the Level a tests and the Level b Tests. When you are ready to administer a Listening subtest, have students turn to the appropriate page in their tests. Read the directions, the reading passages, and the questions, as shown on the following pages. Pause after each question to allow students time to choose their answers. Have students mark their answers on the test page of the Test Answer Document.

Directions for Administering Listening Tests
Midyear Test (Level a)

Have students turn to page 20 in the Midyear Test printout.

Say: *Now you are going to take a listening test. I will read two passages aloud. After each passage, I will read five questions. For each question, you will read the answer choices and choose the best answer. Fill in the circle beside the answer you choose. Here is the first passage. Listen carefully.*

Passage 1: Tornado Warning

With ten minutes left in the school day, everyone was restless. Will looked out the window and saw the buses arriving. Then he saw something else. The sky was an odd greenish-blue. Will gasped. He raised his hand to tell Ms. Baker. But she was already walking to the window to get a better look.

The principal's voice suddenly came over the public address speaker. *The weather service has announced a tornado warning for the county. Everyone should go down to the gym. Please remain calm, but move quickly.*

Will fell into line with Connie and Jim. As they filed down the stairs, they exchanged grim looks. All three of them shared the same worry. It was planting time for farmers. Today their parents were out in their fields sowing corn.

"We shouldn't worry," Will told his friends. "I'm sure they took cover as soon as the warning sirens went off. They're probably in a basement by now, safe and sound, just like us."

Connie and Jim nodded. The sirens made everyone feel safer. The county had installed them eight years ago after a sudden tornado caught farmers by surprise.

The three friends sat together on the gym floor. All they could do was wait.

Questions
Now listen carefully as I read the questions. Choose the best answer to each question and mark your answer.

41.   What happens first in this story?

42.   How does Will feel when he sees the greenish-blue sky?

43.   How does Will treat his friends in this story?

44.   What is the main problem Will and his friends have in this story?

45.   Where are Will and his friends at the end of this story?

Midyear Test (Level a), continued

Now turn to the next page and listen as I read another passage. Then I will read some questions.

Passage 2: Strange Mummies

You may know that the ancient Egyptians often turned human bodies into mummies before burying them. They also mummified cats! In 1888, an Egyptian farmer was digging in the desert. Near a place called Beni Hasan, he found thousands of cat mummies! The farmer had dug up an old pet cemetery. It had been hidden in the ground for over 2,000 years.

The Egyptians were the first people to tame cats. They loved and respected these animals. When a cat died, the cat's owner shaved his eyebrows. That showed how sad he was.

Sometimes a cat was turned into a mummy. The body was placed in a sitting position. Then it was wrapped in a cloth called linen. The linen could be plain white or colorful. Then the mummy was given a mask that looked like a cat face. Many cats were even buried in cat-shaped coffins. The coffins were made of wood or bronze.

Sadly, the cat mummies found at Beni Hasan were not treated with respect. Many of them were sold to tourists. Others were thrown away. Luckily, a few ended up in museums. People can still see them today.

Questions

Now listen carefully as I read the questions. Choose the best answer to each question and mark your answer.

46. What is this passage mostly about?

47. Which event happened first?

48. How did the ancient Egyptians feel about cats?

49. What happened to most of the cat mummies at Beni Hasan?

50. Which sentence best summarizes this passage?

End-of-Year Test (Level a)

Have students turn to page 20 in the End-of-Year Test.

Say: *Now you are going to take a listening test. I will read two passages aloud. After each passage, I will read five questions. For each question, you will read the answer choices and choose the best answer. Fill in the circle beside the answer you choose. Here is the first passage. Listen carefully.*

Passage 1: Reaching for the Top

Today is the day of the rope climb, and I don't think I can do it. Joe Logan, the captain of the soccer team, can climb the rope in about eight seconds. He's in my gym class, but I don't think he knows who I am.

My mom and I moved here from Texas last summer. She still calls me Pedro, but most of the kids call me Pete. When we came here, I thought this school was great. But then I saw the rope climb. The rope hangs from the ceiling in the gym, which is 25 feet high. We have to climb the rope to the top.

"Here goes nothing," I say as I grab the rope.

Mr. Riley looks at his stopwatch and says, "Go!"

I climb the first few feet without too much trouble. I can hear some of the kids yelling to me. As I reach up again, I start to slide. My hands are burning, and my legs start to shake. I have only a few feet to go.

When I reach the top, I am so excited I almost let go of the rope. Then I slowly climb back down. My legs are so tired I can't stand up. Then the bell rings.

As everyone starts leaving, someone pats my back.

"Nice work, Pete," says a voice. It's Joe Logan.

Questions

Now listen carefully as I read the questions. Choose the best answer to each question and mark your answer.

41. Where does this story take place?

42. Which event happens first?

43. What is Pete's problem in this story?

44. What happens at the end of the story?

45. How does Pete probably feel after the rope climb?

End-of-Year Test (Level a), continued

Now turn to the next page and listen as I read another passage. Then I will read some questions.

Passage 2: The Story of the Tomato

Did you ever wonder where tomatoes came from? They are related to potatoes, peppers, and eggplant. But none of these plants is native to the United States. They are also related to a plant called deadly nightshade. It is poisonous. For a long time, some people thought tomatoes were poisonous, too.

Spanish explorers first landed in South America in the early 1500s. They found many plants and foods they had never seen before. In both Peru and Mexico, they found people growing and eating tomatoes. The Spanish took some tomato seeds back to Europe with them.

By the late 1500s, people in Italy, Spain, and France were growing tomato plants for decoration. They were pretty to look at, but people did not eat them. In 1600, tomatoes were being grown in England. But they were considered poisonous. Tomatoes did not become popular as food until almost one hundred years later.

In the 1700s, many people from England and France sailed to the New World and settled in America. Some of them brought tomato seeds with them. Then they could grow tomatoes in their new homes. That's how tomatoes came to America.

Today, we grow and consume millions of tons of tomatoes in the United States every year. It is hard to imagine eating salads, pizza, or spaghetti without them.

Questions

Now listen carefully as I read the questions. Choose the best answer to each question and mark your answer.

46. What is this passage mostly about?

47. Where did tomatoes first come from?

48. How are tomatoes similar to potatoes, peppers, and eggplant?

49. Why did people think that tomatoes were poisonous?

50. Which sentence best summarizes this passage?

Directions for Administering Listening Tests
Midyear Test (Level b)

Have students turn to page 20 in the Midyear Test.

Say: *Now you are going to take a listening test. I will read two passages aloud. After each passage, I will read five questions. For each question, you will read the answer choices and choose the best answer. Fill in the circle beside the answer you choose. Here is the first passage. Listen carefully.*

Passage 1: A Lucky Day

Monday did not start off well. My mother got upset because I didn't get up on time. "Isabel," she warned, "you're going to be late!"

At school we had a math test. Then we got tons of homework.

Mrs. Charles gave us a list of words to look up. So, after school, I went to the town library to use a dictionary.

The first word began with "y." As I paged through the dictionary, a small pile of money suddenly fell out of the W's. For a moment I just stared at it. Then I looked around to see if anyone had noticed, but I was alone. So I counted the bills. I had just found 2,000 dollars!

My friend Leon told me later that I should have kept the money. Darla told me I should have kept at least half of it. But I didn't do either of those things. I marched right up to the librarian's desk and showed her what I had found. She was as shocked as I was, but she told me she would try to find out where the money came from.

On the way home, I wondered if I had done the right thing or not. But then a week later, I got a phone call from the library. They never found out who left the money in the dictionary. The money now belonged to the library and would be used to buy new books. But I got 500 dollars reward for finding the money and being so honest!

Questions
Now listen carefully as I read the questions. Choose the best answer to each question and mark your answer.

41. What does Isabel do first in this story?

42. What problem does Isabel have at home?

43. Where does Isabel find the money?

44. How does Isabel feel when she finds the money?

45. What happens at the end of the story?

Now turn to the next page and listen as I read another passage. Then I will read some questions.

Passage 2: From Costa Rica to Outer Space

Franklin Chang-Diaz was born in 1950 in Costa Rica. His parents named him after Franklin Roosevelt, one of America's greatest presidents.

When Franklin was a boy, he thought a lot about outer space and really wanted to go there. So, he decided to move to the United States to become an astronaut.

Franklin worked hard to make his dream come true. He was an excellent student in Costa Rica. He got a job and saved his money, and in 1968, he moved to Hartford, Connecticut. For a year, Franklin lived with relatives and went to Hartford High School. He struggled at first because he didn't speak English, and his grades were poor. By the end of the year, however, Franklin was a top student. He won a scholarship to study science. He felt sure that his dream would come true.

Franklin studied hard for the next eight years. In 1977, he applied to become an astronaut, but he was turned down. Although Franklin was disappointed, he did not give up. He took a job as a scientist, and he became an American citizen. In 1981, he applied again to become an astronaut. This time, Franklin was chosen. He was the first Latino astronaut in the U.S. space program.

Franklin completed his first space mission in 1986 on the space shuttle *Columbia*. He made six more space flights after that. Franklin left the space program in 2005. Today, he leads a company that works to improve space travel.

Questions

Now listen carefully as I read the questions. Choose the best answer to each question and mark your answer.

46. What is this passage mostly about?

47. Which event happened first?

48. What problem did Franklin face when he first came to the United States?

49. Which detail shows that Franklin did something great with his life?

50. Which sentence best summarizes this passage?

End-of-Year Test (Level b)

Have students turn to page 20 in the End-of-Year Test.

Say: *Now you are going to take a listening test. I will read two passages aloud. After each passage, I will read five questions. For each question, you will read the answer choices and choose the best answer. Fill in the circle beside the answer you choose. Here is the first passage. Listen carefully.*

Passage 1: A New Friend

Kim was quiet as Dad drove her to the mall. She was finally ready to admit to herself that Lizzie didn't want to hang out with her anymore, and that realization hurt a lot.

Kim had seen the signs all summer long but tried to ignore them. The final proof came last night when Lizzie said she didn't want to go back-to-school shopping with Kim. They had been school shopping together since first grade!

As Kim and her dad entered the Super Mart, Kim headed for the school supplies aisle and took out her list. She needed notebooks, pens, pencils, and a calculator. Her stomach began to churn as she thought about going back to school. If Lizzie were there, she would be cracking jokes to make Kim laugh. But Lizzie wasn't there.

Kim stopped in front of the binders and considered which color she should choose. She was reaching for one with a dark blue cover when she heard a voice behind her.

"If you buy that glow-in-the-dark green binder, it might help you stay awake in class," said the voice.

Kim turned around to see Risa Harrison smiling at her. Risa had moved to town last spring, and Kim didn't really know her too well. But their lockers were near each other, and Risa seemed nice.

Kim smiled back at her. "Hey, do you want to help me pick out my school stuff? Then maybe we could get some lunch."

Questions
Now listen carefully as I read the questions. Choose the best answer to each question and mark your answer.

41. Which event happened first?

42. Where does most of this story take place?

43. What was Kim's main problem in this story?

44. What happened at the end of the story?

45. What did Kim and Risa probably do next?

End-of-Year Test (Level b), continued

Now turn to the next page and listen as I read another passage. Then I will read some questions.

Passage 2: Volleyball: Then and Now

In 1895, a man named William Morgan invented the game of volleyball. At the time, Morgan was the director of a YMCA in Massachusetts. He wanted to find a team sport that older men could play at the YMCA. Basketball was a brand-new sport at the time, and it was catching on fast among younger men. Morgan wanted to create a slower, gentler game that was just as much fun as basketball.

Morgan's game of volleyball blended old and new ideas. It uses a court divided by a net, like tennis and badminton. But in place of rackets, volleyball players use their hands to hit a ball over the net.

In 1896, a year after he dreamed up volleyball, Morgan organized a game for other YMCA directors to watch. They liked what they saw. Before long, volleyball was catching on all over the United States. It became a popular team sport in American colleges and high schools because both boys and girls could play. It spread to Europe and Asia. In 1964, it became an official sport of the Olympic Games.

Today, volleyball is one of the most popular team sports in the world. It is also a lot faster and rougher than it was in Morgan's time.

Questions

Now listen carefully as I read the questions. Choose the best answer to each question and mark your answer.

46. What is this passage mostly about?

47. Why did Morgan invent volleyball?

48. When Morgan first invented volleyball, how was it different from basketball?

49. Why did volleyball become a popular team sport in American high schools?

50. Which sentence best summarizes this passage?

Progress Monitoring Assessments:

Below Grade-Level Tests
(Level a)

NAME _____ DATE _____

rSkills® Progress Monitoring Test 1a

DIRECTIONS: This is a reading test. Follow the directions for each part of the test, and choose the best answer to each question.

SAMPLE QUESTIONS

Sample A. Samantha saw a big dog. It looked friendly, but the other children were afraid. Samantha slowly walked up to the dog and its owner.

Samantha was—
Ⓐ afraid.
Ⓑ brave.
Ⓒ weak.
Ⓓ lost.

Sample B. The past tense of *go* is—
Ⓐ goed.
Ⓑ going.
Ⓒ goes.
Ⓓ went.

 See p. 287 for scoring.

Go on to the next page to begin the test.

Comprehension

Read this passage. Then answer questions 1–3 by filling in the circle next to the best answer.

The Los Alamos Fire

Los Alamos is a town in New Mexico. The town is in a beautiful, mountainous area. The mountains are covered with trees. In 2000, these trees almost destroyed the town.

The forest fire of 2000 was started by accident. Forest managers wanted to burn some brush. This is called a prescribed burn. A prescribed burn removes brush and dead trees. Doing this can help prevent a forest fire.

During the burn, the wind picked up and spread the fire. At first, the fire stayed in a canyon. Then it got out of control.

The blaze moved quickly and reached the edge of town. Los Alamos was in danger. More than 18,000 people had to flee. Over 1,000 firefighters did everything they could to put out the fire. In spite of their hard work, the fire destroyed hundreds of homes.

As the fire crept closer to the center of Los Alamos, people fled from nearby towns. Finally, the wind died down and some rain fell. The firefighters got control of the fire. The town of Los Alamos was saved.

A City in Danger

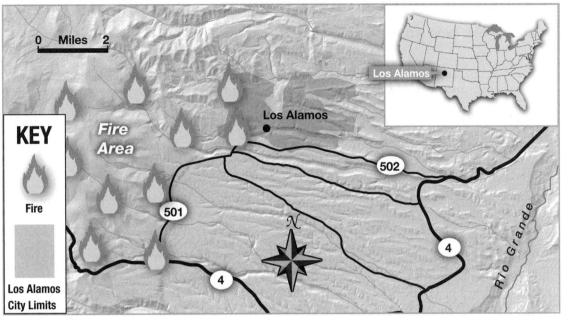

Source: www.geocomm.com (accessed 2/2/05)   Joe LeMonnier

1. This passage is mostly about—

   Ⓐ a town with many forest fires.

   Ⓑ a fire that got out of control.

   Ⓒ rain that helped firefighters.

   Ⓓ winds that can spread a fire.

2. Which event happened *first*?

   Ⓐ People fled Los Alamos.

   Ⓑ The fire destroyed homes.

   Ⓒ Forest managers burned brush.

   Ⓓ Wind spread the fire.

3. According to the map, where did most of the Los Alamos wildfires occur?

   Ⓐ east of Route 501

   Ⓑ west of Route 501

   Ⓒ north of Route 501

   Ⓓ south of Route 501

GO ON

Read this passage. Then answer questions 4–6 by filling in the circle next to the best answer.

Saving the Forest

After the 2000 Los Alamos fire, crews worked quickly. They wanted to save what was left of the forest. Workers also wanted to save the animals that lived there. First, the workers made sure the fire was out. They searched for "hot spots." When they found a hot spot, they soaked it with water.

Next, the workers looked for damaged trees. These trees could cause more danger if they fell. So the workers cut them down. Workers also looked for animals that were hurt in the fire. They took these animals to a special hospital.

Runoff is a problem after a fire. Rain can wash away topsoil in the forest. Crews put logs and rocks in steep areas of the forest. This would keep the soil in place.

As soon as they could, the workers spread grass seed on the forest floor. Grass grows quickly. Grass roots would hold the soil in place.

Finally, the workers planted new trees. The trees were tiny, but they would soon grow. Before long, the forest would be healthy again.

4. What did the crews do *last*?

Ⓐ prevent runoff

Ⓑ look for "hot spots"

Ⓒ save injured animals

Ⓓ plant new trees

5. The workers prevented runoff by—

Ⓐ planting grass seed.

Ⓑ removing animals.

Ⓒ cutting down trees.

Ⓓ soaking hot spots.

6. What did the crews do *first*?

Ⓐ plant grass

Ⓑ place rocks and logs in the forest

Ⓒ look for places where the fire still burned

Ⓓ order new trees for planting

GO ON

Read this passage. Then answer questions 7–10 by filling in the circle next to the best answer.

A Strange New Land

Imagine this: It is about 400 years ago. You and your family live in London, England. London is a big city. One day, you get on a boat. Your family spends weeks crossing the Atlantic Ocean. At last you arrive. The place where you land is called New England.

This new land is strange. It's very different from crowded London. In London there were lots of buildings. But here, in 1600s New England, you see few buildings. In fact, your family must build a house to live in.

At least there is plenty of wood for building. New England is mostly forest. There are trees everywhere. The forests are thick. In some places you can't see more than a few hundred yards away. England has trees, of course. But there aren't many in London. Outside of London, many of the trees have been cut down. That made more room to farm. Farm fields are everywhere.

Even the birds and animals in New England are different. There are huge bears and wild turkeys. A kind of lion roams the forest. Wolves howl at night. It is a strange new world. But soon your family will get used to living here.

7. The main idea of this passage is that—

Ⓐ wild animals are dangerous.

Ⓑ London is a good place to live.

Ⓒ New England is very different from England.

Ⓓ England has lots of farms.

8. According to the passage, how long does it take to cross the Atlantic Ocean?

Ⓐ years

Ⓑ days

Ⓒ months

Ⓓ weeks

9. When the family lands, what do they notice *first*?

Ⓐ few buildings

Ⓑ wood piles

Ⓒ strange animals

Ⓓ farm fields

10. Which animals are *not* mentioned in the passage?

Ⓐ wolves

Ⓑ bears

Ⓒ turkeys

Ⓓ horses

GO ON

Vocabulary/Word Study

Read each question and decide which is the best answer. Fill in the circle next to the answer you have chosen.

11. If you tell a story more than once, you—

Ⓐ untell it.

Ⓑ retell it.

Ⓒ nontell it.

Ⓓ pretell it.

12. Choose the word that has *only* the prefix underlined.

Ⓐ <u>re</u>write

Ⓑ <u>rew</u>rite

Ⓒ <u>r</u>ewrite

Ⓓ rew<u>ri</u>te

13. Which answer could you combine with the suffix *-able* to form a real word?

Ⓐ room

Ⓑ comfort

Ⓒ among

Ⓓ jacket

14. Paper burns easily.
Something that *burns easily* is—

Ⓐ unstable.

Ⓑ fierce.

Ⓒ alive.

Ⓓ flammable.

15. The coach was calm throughout the game, even when we were losing.
The opposite of *calm* is—

Ⓐ upset.

Ⓑ rapid.

Ⓒ slick.

Ⓓ abrupt.

16. Susan smiled at all the familiar people at her birthday party.
Choose the antonym for *familiar*.

Ⓐ unfriendly

Ⓑ unfinished

Ⓒ unimportant

Ⓓ unknown

GO ON

17. Which word means "a person who dreams"?

(A) dreaming

(B) dreams

(C) dreamer

(D) dreamed

18. Tari jogs every day and goes to the gym frequently.
Choose the synonym for *frequently*.

(A) kindly

(B) often

(C) rarely

(D) never

19. The voyage to America took four weeks.
What is a *voyage*?

(A) a journey

(B) an airplane

(C) a letter

(D) a job

20. Mr. Richards wants to be governor.
The word *governor* means—

(A) govern again.

(B) not governed.

(C) one who governs.

(D) before governing.

Grammar, Usage, and Mechanics

Read each question and decide which is the best answer. Fill in the circle next to the answer you have chosen.

21. Which answer is a fragment, not a sentence?

Ⓐ Many flowers are growing.

Ⓑ Fish swam in the pond.

Ⓒ The pond in the garden.

Ⓓ The garden is over there.

22. Which sentence has correct end punctuation?

Ⓐ The party is over,

Ⓑ The party is over.

Ⓒ Is the party over.

Ⓓ Is the party over

23. Read this sentence fragment. Which is the best way to correct it?
Rode her bicycle to the store.

Ⓐ The store rode her bicycle to my sister.

Ⓑ My sister rode her bicycle to the store.

Ⓒ Rode to the store my sister her bicycle.

Ⓓ Her bicycle to the store rode my sister.

24. Which sentence has correct capitalization?

Ⓐ Brick houses are very strong.

Ⓑ brick houses are very Strong.

Ⓒ Brick Houses are very strong.

Ⓓ brick houses are very strong.

GO ON

25. Which of these is a complete sentence?

   Ⓐ On the side of the road.

   Ⓑ The sun was hot.

   Ⓒ Driving across the desert.

   Ⓓ No trees or flowers.

26. Which sentence should end with a question mark?

   Ⓐ That boy is my brother

   Ⓑ We live in Santa Ana

   Ⓒ It is near the ocean

   Ⓓ Where do you live

27. Read this sentence fragment. Which is the best way to correct it?

   Three girls in the park.

   Ⓐ Three girls played basketball in the park.

   Ⓑ In the park three girls.

   Ⓒ Three girls and two boys in the park.

   Ⓓ On Saturday, three girls in the park.

28. Which sentence uses capital letters correctly?

   Ⓐ We went to long beach yesterday.

   Ⓑ We went to Long beach yesterday.

   Ⓒ We went to Long Beach yesterday.

   Ⓓ We went to Long Beach Yesterday.

29. Which is a simple sentence?

Ⓐ Those girls listen to music all the time.

Ⓑ Hieran likes rap, but Lisa likes jazz.

Ⓒ Many different kinds of music.

Ⓓ They know all the songs, and they like to dance.

30. Which of these is a compound sentence?

Ⓐ My dad has a vegetable garden.

Ⓑ He rakes the soil, and I plant the seeds.

Ⓒ Carrots, beans, and peas grow well.

Ⓓ Dad waters the garden and picks the vegetables.

GO ON

Open Response

Go back to the passages on pages 2 and 6 to answer these questions. Write your answers in your own words. Use complete sentences.

31. Look at the passage "The Los Alamos Fire." Write one or two sentences to describe what happened right after the wind picked up.

_____

_____

_____

_____

32. Look at the passage "A Strange New Land." Why were there so few trees around London? Write one or two sentences.

_____

_____

_____

_____

Writing

Read the prompt. Write your essay on the lines below. If you need more space, continue writing on separate paper.

Explain how firefighters and police officers help people in your city or town.

When you write your essay, remember to
- state the main topic,
- include details that support the main idea, and
- use correct grammar, spelling, punctuation, and capitalization.

_____

_____

_____

_____

_____

_____

_____

_____

_____

rSkills® Progress Monitoring
Test 2a

DIRECTIONS: This is a reading test. Follow the directions for each part of the test, and choose the best answer to each question.

SAMPLE QUESTIONS

Sample A. Ken told his mother that he would be home late after school. He was going to a meeting of the science club.

Where was Ken going after school?

Ⓐ to a meeting

Ⓑ to a game

Ⓒ to the library

Ⓓ to the park

Sample B. Which word means the same as *noisy*?

Ⓐ ugly

Ⓑ silly

Ⓒ loud

Ⓓ pushy

See p. 288 for scoring.

Go on to the next page to begin the test.

Comprehension

Read this passage. Then answer questions 1–4 by filling in the circle next to the best answer.

Working It Out

Like adults, children don't always agree. Some children get into fights. Schools now teach kids ways to work things out. Instead of fighting, children learn to solve problems together. One way is through mediation.

Mediation can help children to talk without hurting each other. Schools train some children to be peer mediators. A peer mediator is a peacemaker. When students have a problem, the peacemakers help out. One way is by asking questions. This gets the students who disagree to talk about what is going on.

Schools also teach children to use words instead of fists. That way, kids will talk instead of hitting each other.

Teaching respect is another way that schools help children to get along. Students learn to be kind to each other. They try to see each other's strengths. They also learn how hurtful words can be. When children are respectful, fighting is less likely.

Finally, schools teach kids how to work together. Kids are put on teams. This is called team building. The teams compete. Team building may sound hard, but it's fun! Children who work together on a team get to know each other. This helps them to get along.

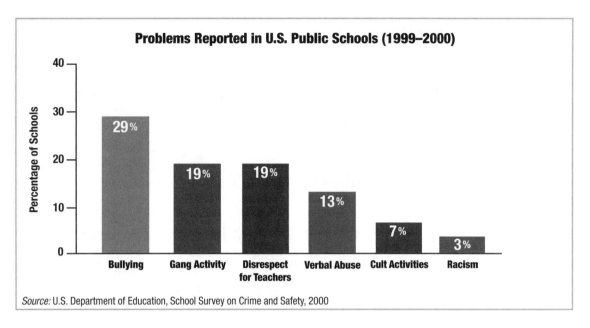

Problems Reported in U.S. Public Schools (1999–2000)

Source: U.S. Department of Education, School Survey on Crime and Safety, 2000

1. Choose the sentence that best summarizes the passage.

Ⓐ Teachers break up a lot of fights.

Ⓑ All children should be peer mediators.

Ⓒ Children at school often disagree.

Ⓓ Schools teach children how to solve problems.

2. Which way of solving problems does the passage mention *second*?

Ⓐ using words, not fists

Ⓑ training children to be mediators

Ⓒ teaching children to respect each other

Ⓓ putting children on teams

GO ON

3. Which sentence best summarizes the last paragraph?

    Ⓐ Schools teach children to respect each other.

    Ⓑ Schools train children to talk about their disagreements.

    Ⓒ Schools help children to get along by teaching several kinds of mediation.

    Ⓓ Schools teach children to get along by working in teams.

4. Look at the bar graph on page 3. Which two problems exist in the same percentage of schools?

    Ⓐ gang activity and disrespect for teachers

    Ⓑ disrespect for teachers and verbal abuse

    Ⓒ gang activity and racism

    Ⓓ bullying and gang activity

Read this passage. Then answer questions 5–10 by filling in the circle next to the best answer.

Hard Times

"You be careful with those shoes!" Mother warned Johnny with a smile.

Johnny nodded. There was little money these days. The Anson family grew or made almost everything they needed to live. It was the only way to survive.

Johnny headed toward the barn. Skeeter, the family dog, was at his side.

Mr. Anson had already milked the cows. He needed Johnny's help carrying the milk cans back to the house. Some of the milk was for drinking. The rest would be made into cheese or butter.

"Where have you been, sleepyhead?" Karen stuck her tongue out at her younger brother. She had helped her father with the milking. Now she was gathering eggs from the chickens.

"I was resting," Johnny replied. "That copper I brought back from the Smiths' place was heavy."

The night before, Johnny had walked more than a mile to the Smiths' farm. He carried several dozen eggs. He traded the eggs for sheets of copper. His father would use the copper to make buckets.

Times were hard all over the country. The Great Depression was on. Banks were closing. There were few jobs. Most families worked hard like the Ansons. People did what they could to get by.

GO ON

5. Which sentence best summarizes how the Anson family is surviving the Great Depression?

Ⓐ They trade eggs for copper.

Ⓑ They grow or make what they need.

Ⓒ They make butter and cheese.

Ⓓ They have a vegetable garden.

6. Karen teased Johnny because—

Ⓐ he had dropped some eggs.

Ⓑ he was late.

Ⓒ he had spilled the milk.

Ⓓ he had lost the copper.

7. Johnny was—

Ⓐ lazy.

Ⓑ strong.

Ⓒ weak.

Ⓓ silly.

8. Where does this story take place?

Ⓐ by the creek

Ⓑ on the Smith farm

Ⓒ in the tractor shed

Ⓓ on the Anson farm

9. Why did the Ansons trade with the Smiths?

Ⓐ They had too many eggs.

Ⓑ They liked copper.

Ⓒ They didn't have money to buy things.

Ⓓ The Smiths were good neighbors.

10. During what time in American history does this story take place?

Ⓐ during a mining disaster

Ⓑ during colonial times

Ⓒ during the Civil War

Ⓓ during the Great Depression

GO ON

Vocabulary/Word Study

Read each question and decide which is the best answer. Fill in the circle next to the answer you have chosen.

11. Choose the word that is *not* in the same family as the others.

Ⓐ clearing

Ⓑ cleaned

Ⓒ clear

Ⓓ clearly

12. Which pair of words are homophones?

Ⓐ steal/steel

Ⓑ fed/feed

Ⓒ grain/grown

Ⓓ nearly/nearby

13. The sound was so faint that rescue workers barely heard it. In this sentence, *faint* means—

Ⓐ weak.

Ⓑ musical.

Ⓒ unaware.

Ⓓ pale.

14. The museum keeps precious jewelry in a glass case.
In this sentence, *precious* means—

Ⓐ family.

Ⓑ beautiful.

Ⓒ antique.

Ⓓ valuable.

15. Which of these words is a compound word?

Ⓐ pattern

Ⓑ scenery

Ⓒ roadside

Ⓓ mountain

16. Which word can you combine with *jelly* to form a compound word?

Ⓐ belly

Ⓑ fish

Ⓒ gum

Ⓓ bear

17. Choose the word that best fits in the sentence.

Nate likes strawberry ice cream, but he _____ chocolate.

Ⓐ preference

Ⓑ prefers

Ⓒ preferably

Ⓓ offering

GO ON

18. Choose the word that best fits in the sentence.

There were _____ people waiting in line.

Ⓐ for

Ⓑ fore

Ⓒ fur

Ⓓ four

19. Lenny was ravenous after not eating for two days. In this sentence, *ravenous* means—

Ⓐ sleepy.

Ⓑ upset.

Ⓒ hungry.

Ⓓ nervous.

20. Which word can you combine with *cross* to form a compound word?

Ⓐ walk

Ⓑ trade

Ⓒ door

Ⓓ speak

Grammar, Usage, and Mechanics

Read each question and decide which is the best answer. Fill in the circle next to the answer you have chosen.

21. How would you correct this run-on sentence?

We walked along the trail it goes by the river.

Ⓐ We walked. Along the trail it goes by the river.

Ⓑ We walked along the trail it goes. By the river.

Ⓒ We walked along the trail and it goes by the river.

Ⓓ We walked along the trail that goes by the river.

22. In which sentence is the verb tense correct?

Ⓐ Yesterday my friend tells me a secret.

Ⓑ He like to take walks in the park.

Ⓒ Mom parked the car near the gym.

Ⓓ Jeremy play badminton when he was young.

23. Which sentence has correct word order?

Ⓐ He walked quickly to the park this morning.

Ⓑ To the park walked quickly he this morning.

Ⓒ This morning to the park quickly he walked.

Ⓓ This morning to the park he walked quickly.

24. Which sentence shows the correct use of commas?

Ⓐ We had milk toast and fruit, for breakfast.

Ⓑ We had, milk, toast, and fruit for breakfast.

Ⓒ We had milk, toast, and fruit for breakfast.

Ⓓ We had milk toast, and fruit for breakfast.

GO ON

25. Which is the best way to correct this run-on sentence?

Tami got on the train her dad waved goodbye.

Ⓐ Tami got on. The train her dad waved goodbye.

Ⓑ Tami got on the train. Her dad waved goodbye.

Ⓒ Tami got on the train her dad. Waved goodbye.

Ⓓ Tami got on the train that her dad waved goodbye.

26. In which sentence is the word order correct?

Ⓐ He looking was under the bed for his shoes.

Ⓑ For his shoes he was under the bed looking.

Ⓒ Looking for his shoes under the bed he was.

Ⓓ He was looking under the bed for his shoes.

27. Which sentence uses the correct verb tense?

Ⓐ Last week Mom take the bus to work.

Ⓑ Her car breaks down six days ago.

Ⓒ On Monday she went to the auto shop.

Ⓓ She decide to leave the car there.

28. In which sentence are commas used correctly?

Ⓐ Fredo likes fishing, camping, and sailing.

Ⓑ Fredo likes, fishing, camping, and sailing.

Ⓒ Fredo likes fishing, camping, and, sailing.

Ⓓ Fredo likes, fishing camping, and sailing.

29. Read these sentences.

> Max wrote a song about rainbows.
> It was a beautiful song.

How can these sentences *best* be joined without changing the meaning?

Ⓐ Max wrote a song about rainbows, and it was a beautiful song.

Ⓑ Max wrote a song about beautiful rainbows.

Ⓒ Max wrote a beautiful song it was about rainbows.

Ⓓ Max wrote a beautiful song about rainbows.

30. Read these sentences.

> Judith lives in Fresno.
> Judith is my cousin.

What is the *best* way to combine these sentences?

Ⓐ Judith lives in Fresno she is my cousin.

Ⓑ My cousin Judith lives in Fresno.

Ⓒ Judith lives in Fresno and is my cousin.

Ⓓ In Fresno Judith lives, my cousin.

GO ON

Open Response

Go back to the passages on pages 2 and 5 to answer these questions. Write your answers in your own words. Use complete sentences.

31. Look at the passage "Working It Out." Write a two-sentence summary of how team building works.

_____

_____

_____

_____

32. Look at the story "Hard Times." How can you tell that the story takes place on a farm? Write one or two sentences.

_____

_____

_____

_____

Writing

Read the prompt. Write your essay on the lines below. If you need more space, continue writing on separate paper.

You read the story "Hard Times" (on page 5). You may want to read it again. What did you learn from reading this story? Use details from the story to support your answer.

When you write your essay, remember to
- show your understanding of the story,
- give examples from the story, and
- use correct grammar, spelling, punctuation, and capitalization.

_____

_____

_____

_____

_____

_____

_____

_____

rSkills® Progress Monitoring
Test 3a

DIRECTIONS: This is a reading test. Follow the directions for each part of the test, and choose the best answer to each question.

SAMPLE QUESTIONS

Sample A. Which pair of words are homophones?

Ⓐ one/own

Ⓑ me/my

Ⓒ for/four

Ⓓ went/want

Sample B. Mike was so excited when the team won that he jumped up and down.

Which word means the opposite of *excited*?

Ⓐ busy   Ⓒ cold

Ⓑ calm   Ⓓ unhappy

See p. 289 for scoring.

Go on to the next page to begin the test.

Comprehension

Read this passage. Then answer questions 1–4 by filling in the circle next to the best answer.

Children in Ancient Egypt

What was it like growing up in Ancient Egypt? There are no history books from that time. However, ancient art gives us clues about children's lives back then.

Egyptian children played with toys. They had dolls, balls, and wooden animals. They also played board games. Some children had pets like kittens or dogs.

The children worked and helped their parents. Mothers taught their daughters how to do chores at home. A father who knew a craft might teach it to his son. Boys also worked in the fields with their fathers. Some boys started working at age four.

Children from royal families learned reading, writing, and math at home. Wealthy boys went to school. Some parents were poor and could not afford to send their sons to school. Most girls did not go to school. However, girls might learn to read and write at home, and some even became doctors.

Life was dangerous for children in Ancient Egypt. Many babies died soon after birth. Babies wore lucky charms to protect them. Parents also said spells to keep their children safe and healthy.

Childhood in Ancient Egypt did not last long. Most children married by age 12 or 14. Often, their parents chose who they would marry.

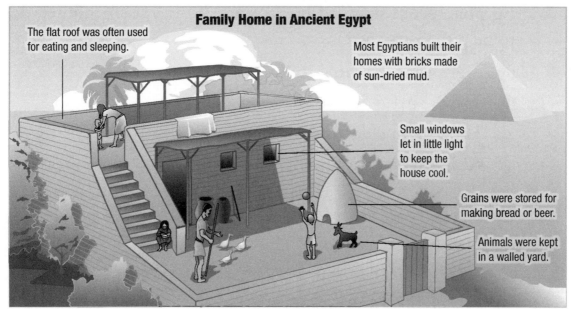

Family Home in Ancient Egypt

The flat roof was often used for eating and sleeping.

Most Egyptians built their homes with bricks made of sun-dried mud.

Small windows let in little light to keep the house cool.

Grains were stored for making bread or beer.

Animals were kept in a walled yard.

Source: University of Minnesota eMuseum

Tim Pack

1. Which sentence gives the best summary of the passage?

Ⓐ Children in Ancient Egypt were often sick.

Ⓑ Children in Ancient Egypt played with kittens.

Ⓒ Children in Ancient Egypt were wealthy.

Ⓓ Children in Ancient Egypt played and worked.

2. Keeping children healthy was a problem. How did parents try to solve this problem?

Ⓐ They made their children marry young.

Ⓑ They sent their children to school.

Ⓒ They gave their babies charms to wear.

Ⓓ They made their children read spells aloud.

GO ON

3. Egyptian parents needed help. What did Egyptian children do to help their parents?

  Ⓐ They went to school to learn a craft.

  Ⓑ They married at a young age.

  Ⓒ They became doctors.

  Ⓓ Girls did chores at home, and boys worked in the fields.

4. Look at the diagram. How did the family solve the problem of keeping their animals safe?

  Ⓐ They built a flat roof.

  Ⓑ They built a wall around their yard.

  Ⓒ They kept their animals indoors.

  Ⓓ They watched the animals through a window.

Read this passage. Then answer questions 5–10 by filling in the circle next to the best answer.

First Lesson

When Diana was 12, she lost her leg. She had bone cancer. Doctors removed her leg to keep the disease from spreading.

It took more than a year for Diana to get better. Slowly, she learned to use crutches. Then, she got an artificial leg. Soon she could walk again.

Diana missed playing soccer, however. She thought her sports days were over. She was in for a surprise. Her mother took her to the National Sports Center for the Disabled. Diana was going to learn to ski.

Diana had her doubts. "I've never skied before!" she wailed.

"You'll learn," her mom said with a smile. "You can do it!"

At the center, Diana saw lots of people. Many had artificial limbs. Some were in wheelchairs. Others were blind. They were all there for sports.

A girl on crutches smiled at Diana. "I'm Emma," the girl said. "Going skiing?"

"It's my first time," Diana told her.

"The snow is awesome!" Emma said.

An instructor helped Diana remove her artificial leg. He put a ski boot on her other foot. Diana struggled to stand up. She had special ski poles for support.

While riding the ski lift, Diana studied the scene below. The slopes were filled with skiers. Some were just learning. A few were quite good.

The lift stopped at the top of the hill. Maybe I can do this, Diana thought.

GO ON

5. What is the theme of this story?

 Ⓐ meeting new friends   Ⓒ overcoming difficulty

 Ⓑ getting hurt   Ⓓ avoiding sadness

6. Diana's mother brought her to the Sports Center to—

 Ⓐ learn to ski.   Ⓒ get an artificial leg.

 Ⓑ meet other disabled people.   Ⓓ ride a ski lift.

7. Emma probably spoke to Diana because—

 Ⓐ she wanted to teach Diana how to ski.

 Ⓑ she wanted to ski with Diana.

 Ⓒ she wanted to be friends.

 Ⓓ she wanted to show Diana where the ski lift was.

8. How would you describe Diana's mother?

 Ⓐ She believed in Diana.

 Ⓑ She bossed Diana around.

 Ⓒ She was angry at Diana.

 Ⓓ She was afraid Diana would get hurt.

9. Where does the end of the story take place?

 Ⓐ on an ice rink   Ⓒ at a hospital

 Ⓑ inside the Center   Ⓓ on a ski lift

10. Which sentence best states how Diana felt at the end of the story?

 Ⓐ She was afraid of the ski lift.

 Ⓑ She was somewhat confident.

 Ⓒ She was sure she couldn't ski.

 Ⓓ She was angry at her instructor.

Vocabulary/Word Study

Read each question and decide which is the best answer. Fill in the circle next to the answer you have chosen.

11. A homophone for *pail* is—

Ⓒ pal.

Ⓑ pale.

Ⓔ pole.

Ⓕ peel.

12. Which pair of words are homophones?

Ⓒ shed/sled

Ⓑ hole/while

Ⓔ real/reel

Ⓕ toad/toes

13. What does the idiom "a piece of cake" mean in this sentence?

The test was *a piece of cake*, so Brad passed it easily.

Ⓒ Something is easy.

Ⓑ You are hungry.

Ⓔ Something is ready to microwave.

Ⓕ You are cooking.

GO ON

14. What does the idiom "get it" mean in this sentence?

I really *get it* when Mr. Parker explains geometry.

Ⓐ forget it

Ⓑ don't like it

Ⓒ confused by it

Ⓓ understand it

15. Choose the word that is in the same word family as *true*.

Ⓐ tree

Ⓑ truck

Ⓒ truth

Ⓓ truce

16. Which word fits best in both sentences?

Our school had a _____ to raise money.

We chose sides to make the game _____.

Ⓐ sale

Ⓑ fair

Ⓒ equal

Ⓓ picnic

17. Choose the word that best fits in the sentence.

On Friday, Dan _____ his bike to school.

Ⓐ road

Ⓑ rode

Ⓒ rude

Ⓓ rowed

18. What does the idiom "hit the roof" mean in this sentence?

When Mom saw the D on my report card, she *hit the roof.*

Ⓐ got angry

Ⓑ jumped high

Ⓒ felt happy

Ⓓ stood up

19. Choose the word that best fits in the sentence.

We waited for the singers to _____ on the stage.

Ⓐ pear

Ⓑ appear

Ⓒ disappear

Ⓓ appearance

20. Which word fits best in both sentences?

I used my new _____ to write a note.

Mr. Cole keeps his dogs in a _____.

Ⓐ marker

Ⓑ cage

Ⓒ yard

Ⓓ pen

GO ON

Grammar, Usage, and Mechanics

Read each question and decide which is the best answer. Fill in the circle next to the answer you have chosen.

21. Choose the word that fits best in this sentence.

The plane _____ across the ocean.

Ⓐ flew

Ⓑ flied

Ⓒ fly

Ⓓ flown

22. Which sentence shows the correct use of commas?

Ⓐ Tina don't, forget your backpack.

Ⓑ Tina, don't forget your backpack.

Ⓒ Tina don't forget your, backpack.

Ⓓ Tina don't forget, your backpack.

23. Look at the underlined part of each sentence. Which sentence is correct?

Ⓐ The <u>puppy like</u> to sleep under the bed.

Ⓑ The <u>puppies likes</u> to sleep under the bed.

Ⓒ The <u>puppies like</u> to sleep under the bed.

Ⓓ The <u>puppy liking</u> to sleep under the bed.

24. Choose the word that fits best in the sentence.

The students in the class had a party for their math _____ birthday.

Ⓐ teachers

Ⓑ teacher's

Ⓒ teachers's

Ⓓ teachers'

25. Choose the word that fits best in this sentence.

Last week, Aza _____ some old coins in his yard.

Ⓐ find

Ⓑ finded

Ⓒ finding

Ⓓ found

26. Which sentence needs a comma after the first word?

Ⓐ Sean wants to buy some new shoes.

Ⓑ Does he have a pair of sneakers?

Ⓒ No he does not like sneakers.

Ⓓ Maybe Sean will get some sandals.

27. Which sentence is written correctly?

Ⓐ Petra's brother making breakfast every morning.

Ⓑ Petra's brother makes breakfast every morning.

Ⓒ Petra's brother make breakfast every morning.

Ⓓ Petra's brothers makes breakfast every morning.

GO ON

28. Choose the word that fits best in the sentence.

My _____ house has a gray roof.

Ⓐ uncle

Ⓑ uncles

Ⓒ uncles'

Ⓓ uncle's

29. Read this sentence.

Lynn wants to go to the concert, _____ she does not have a ticket.

Which word would *best* connect the two parts of this sentence?

Ⓐ or

Ⓑ so

Ⓒ but

Ⓓ because

30. Which sentence is written correctly?

Ⓐ Abel made some fish tacos because they tasted pretty good.

Ⓑ Abel made some fish tacos, however they tasted pretty good.

Ⓒ Abel made some fish tacos, though they tasted pretty good.

Ⓓ Abel made some fish tacos; in addition, they tasted pretty good.

Open Response

**Go back to the passages on pages 2 and 5 to answer these questions.
Write your answers in your own words. Use complete sentences.**

---

31. Look at the passage "Children in Ancient Egypt." What
problems did Egyptian children have? Write one or two
sentences describing their problems.

_____

_____

_____

_____

---

32. Look at the story "First Lesson." How do you think Diana felt
when she got her artificial leg? Write one or two sentences.

_____

_____

_____

_____

GO ON

Writing

Read the prompt. Write your essay on the lines below. If you need more space, continue writing on separate paper.

Write an essay to persuade your parent(s) that you should get a pet.

When you write your essay, remember to
- state your opinion,
- give reasons to support your opinion, and
- use correct grammar, spelling, punctuation, and capitalization.

_____

_____

_____

_____

_____

_____

_____

_____

_____

_____

rSkills® Progress Monitoring Test 4a

DIRECTIONS: This is a reading test. Follow the directions for each part of the test, and choose the best answer to each question.

SAMPLE QUESTIONS

Sample A. Which pair of words is in the same word family?

Ⓐ sing/sink

Ⓑ pen/penny

Ⓒ help/helpful

Ⓓ bus/busy

Sample B. Which word is a compound word?

Ⓐ common

Ⓑ lightning

Ⓒ remain

Ⓓ bedroom

See p. 290 for scoring.

Go on to the next page to begin the test.

Comprehension

Read this passage. Then answer questions 1–5 by filling in the circle next to the best answer.

Animal Watching

Where can you see wild animals? If you live near a wooded area, you might see deer in your yard.

You can also spot wild animals at a local park. Get an adult to go with you to the park at night or early in the morning. You are likely to see more animals then. Be very still, however. Most animals are afraid of people!

A zoo is a good place for animal watchers. Some cities have huge zoos. A zoo may have rare animals. Zoo animals live in enclosed areas. People stay outside of those areas. This keeps the people and the animals safe.

Some animal watchers take trips. One place they go is Kenya. Unusual animals like lions and zebras live there.

1. Choose the sentence that best summarizes the passage.
   Ⓐ Animals like to hang out in parks.
   Ⓑ Most wild animals live in zoos.
   Ⓒ There are many places to see wild animals.
   Ⓓ Wild animals are dangerous.

2. Why is the night a good time to look for animals in a park?
   Ⓐ The animals sleep all day.
   Ⓑ Animals come out when people aren't around.
   Ⓒ Animals see better in the dark.
   Ⓓ The animals are less dangerous.

3. According to the passage, if you make a sudden movement near a park animal, it will probably—

Ⓐ come toward you.

Ⓑ beg for food.

Ⓒ run away.

Ⓓ walk away.

4. How are zoo animals different from animals that live in a park?

Ⓐ Zoo animals live in closed spaces.

Ⓑ Zoo animals are free to go anywhere they want.

Ⓒ Zoo animals have to catch their food.

Ⓓ Zoo animals are happier.

5. People go to Kenya to see wild animals because—

Ⓐ the animals in Kenya are friendlier.

Ⓑ they like to travel far.

Ⓒ the animals in Kenya are more unusual.

Ⓓ they want to see animals that are in zoos.

GO ON

Read this passage. Then answer questions 6–10 by filling in the circle next to the best answer.

The Children's Garden

A school in California has a special garden. Alice Waters, a famous cook, made it. The garden is a place to learn. Here children find out about food.

Children help plant the garden. First, they get the soil ready. Then they plant many kinds of seeds. Many farmers use chemicals to grow their crops. The children use only natural things to help their garden grow.

The children also cook the food they grow. A chef teaches them how. The chef shows kids how to cook foods they already eat. They also learn about new foods.

Children today eat too much fast food. Alice Waters cares about children and wants them to be healthy. She teaches kids to make smarter food choices. Children learn to eat more fruits and vegetables. They also learn to stay away from foods that are bad for them.

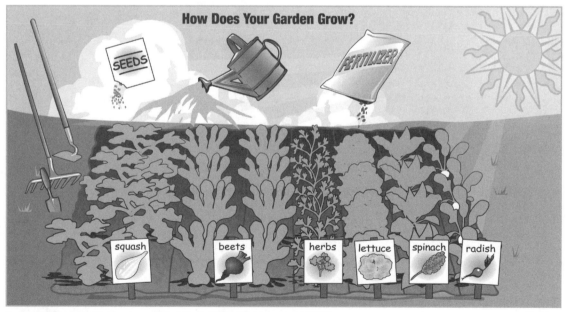

Source: http://aggie-horticulture.tamu.edu/nutrition/schoolgardens/ (accessed 1/19/05)   Tim Pack

6. Why did Alice Waters start her garden?

   Ⓐ to get good vegetables for her restaurant

   Ⓑ to teach kids about food

   Ⓒ to help students get better grades

   Ⓓ to feed poor people

7. According to the passage, how is the school garden different from a regular farm?

   Ⓐ It is in California.

   Ⓑ It only grows tomatoes.

   Ⓒ It charges more for food.

   Ⓓ It does not use chemicals.

8. Alice Waters hopes that growing their own food will help children—

   Ⓐ make smart food choices.

   Ⓑ become farmers.

   Ⓒ go to college.

   Ⓓ start a restaurant.

9. What problem is stated in the passage?

   Ⓐ Kids don't know how to cook.

   Ⓑ Kids do not get enough exercise.

   Ⓒ Kids eat too much fruit.

   Ⓓ Kids eat too much fast food.

GO ON

10. Look at the diagram of the garden on page 4. Which of these statements is true?

Ⓐ Beets take up less space than herbs.

Ⓑ Spinach takes up about the same space as squash.

Ⓒ Lettuce takes up about the same space as beets.

Ⓓ Squash takes up about the same space as beets.

Vocabulary/Word Study

Read each question and decide which is the best answer. Fill in the circle next to the answer you have chosen.

11. It is usual for the days to grow longer during summer.
A word that means about the same as *usual* is—

Ⓐ infrequent.

Ⓑ common.

Ⓒ unreal.

Ⓓ unusual.

12. Which word fits both sentences best?

Tonette _____ a bird in a tree.

Rasheed used a _____ to cut the wood.

Ⓐ saw

Ⓑ earned

Ⓒ built

Ⓓ scored

13. Which verb correctly fits this sentence?

The rabbit _____ across the lawn.

Ⓐ hoping

Ⓑ hoped

Ⓒ hopped

Ⓓ hopping

GO ON

14. Which underlined verb has the correct verb ending?

Ⓐ It has been <u>snow</u> all day.

Ⓑ It has been <u>snowing</u> all day.

Ⓒ It has been <u>snowed</u> all day.

Ⓓ It has been <u>snows</u> all day.

15. Which answer can you combine with the suffix *-ful* to form a real word?

Ⓐ today

Ⓑ brown

Ⓒ call

Ⓓ care

16. Which word would you find on a dictionary page with the guide words *bin* and *bite*?

Ⓐ birthday

Ⓑ bill

Ⓒ bitter

Ⓓ black

17. The polar bear slipped on the ice and tumbled into the water. Which word means about the same as *tumbled*?

Ⓐ fell

Ⓑ looked

Ⓒ swam

Ⓓ drank

18. Which word best fits in both sentences?

The _____ swims fast to catch a fish.

Mr. Brown used some tape to _____ the box.

Ⓐ close

Ⓑ shark

Ⓒ seal

Ⓓ wrap

19. Which of these can be combined with the suffix *-able* to form a real word?

Ⓐ soon

Ⓑ yellow

Ⓒ feel

Ⓓ agree

20. Which word would you find on a dictionary page with the guide words *mellow* and *mercy*?

Ⓐ meet

Ⓑ menu

Ⓒ messy

Ⓓ metal

GO ON

Grammar, Usage, and Mechanics

Read each question and decide which is the best answer. Fill in the circle next to the answer you have chosen.

21. Choose the pronoun that best fits the sentence.

Tomoko and Minda are late. _____ were stuck in traffic.

Ⓐ Them

Ⓑ They

Ⓒ Their

Ⓓ Theirs

22. How would you correct this sentence?

There isn't no juice in the refrigerator.

Ⓐ There isn't not juice in the refrigerator.

Ⓑ There isn't none juice in the refrigerator.

Ⓒ There isn't any juice in the refrigerator.

Ⓓ There isn't not any juice in the refrigerator.

23. Choose the sentence with the correct underlined word.

Ⓐ This room is too <u>large</u> than the others.

Ⓑ This room is <u>largest</u> than the others.

Ⓒ This room is <u>large</u> than the others.

Ⓓ This room is <u>larger</u> than the others.

24. Which sentence uses quotation marks correctly?

Ⓐ Mom asked, "When will you be home from school?"

Ⓑ Mom asked, When will you be home from school?

Ⓒ "Mom asked, When will you be home from school?"

Ⓓ Mom asked, "When will you be home from school?

25. Choose the word that best fits in the sentence.

Jimmy and I were hungry. Dad made sandwiches for _____.

Ⓐ it

Ⓑ them

Ⓒ him

Ⓓ us

26. Which sentence is written correctly?

Ⓐ Gina never goes to the zoo.

Ⓑ Gina doesn't never go to the zoo.

Ⓒ Gina doesn't not ever go to the zoo.

Ⓓ Gina does not never go to the zoo.

27. Choose the word that best fits in the sentence.

Leon is the _____ person I know.

Ⓐ funny

Ⓑ funnier

Ⓒ funnily

Ⓓ funniest

GO ON

28. Which sentence uses quotation marks correctly?

Ⓐ I don't eat eggs or cheese, said Pamela.

Ⓑ "I don't eat eggs or cheese," said Pamela.

Ⓒ "I don't eat eggs or cheese, said Pamela."

Ⓓ I don't eat eggs or cheese, "said Pamela."

29. Read these two sentences.

> Kanye had to stay after school. He did not turn in his homework.

Which word could *best* be used to join these sentences?

Ⓐ or

Ⓑ but

Ⓒ because

Ⓓ while

30. What is the correct way to write this sentence?

Tyra bought some peaches, being delicious.

Ⓐ Tyra bought some peaches and were being delicious.

Ⓑ Tyra bought some peaches, which were delicious.

Ⓒ Tyra bought some peaches, they being delicious.

Ⓓ Tyra bought some peaches, who were being delicious.

Open Response

**Go back to the passages on pages 2 and 4 to answer these questions.
Write your answers in your own words. Use complete sentences.**

---

31. Look at the passage "Animal Watching." Write one or two sentences
to explain why you might go to a zoo instead of a local park to see a
wild animal from Africa.

_____

_____

_____

_____

---

32. Look at the passage "The Children's Garden." How is Alice Waters's
garden different from most gardens?

_____

_____

_____

_____

GO ON

Writing

Read the prompt. Write your essay on the lines below. If you need more space, continue writing on separate paper.

Describe a park or playground near your home, or one that you have seen.

When you write your description, remember to
- tell what you are describing,
- use details to make your description interesting, and
- use correct grammar, spelling, punctuation, and capitalization.

_____

_____

_____

_____

_____

_____

_____

_____

_____

_____

rSkills® Progress Monitoring Test 5a

DIRECTIONS: This is a reading test. Follow the directions for each part of the test, and choose the best answer to each question.

SAMPLE QUESTIONS

Sample A. Which ending would you add to the verb *stay* to make it past tense?

Ⓐ -d

Ⓑ -ed

Ⓒ -ied

Ⓓ -ing

Sample B. Emma told her mother that she would be home late after school. She was going to visit her friend Li Mei.

Where was Emma going after school?

Ⓐ to her friend's house

Ⓑ to the mall

Ⓒ to the library

Ⓓ to the park

See p. 291 for scoring.

Go on to the next page to begin the test.

Comprehension

Read this passage. Then answer questions 1–5 by filling in the circle next to the best answer.

Leading the Way

Elizabeth Blackwell was born in England in 1821. Her family moved to the United States. Elizabeth was just ten years old. Young Elizabeth became interested in medicine. She wanted to help women with their health problems.

Elizabeth tried to go to medical school. Only men could become doctors then. Elizabeth studied medicine on her own. She tried to get into many medical schools. They all said no. Finally, Geneva Medical College in New York said yes.

At first, many students and teachers did not want Elizabeth at the school. Elizabeth worked hard. In time, students and teachers were impressed by her ability. She graduated first in her class. In 1849, Elizabeth became the first woman to earn a medical degree.

Life was still hard for Elizabeth. Many hospitals would not hire her. She started caring for women and children from her home. Then, she opened her own hospital. Many years later, Elizabeth set up the first medical school for women. She worked in medicine all her life. She received many honors for her work.

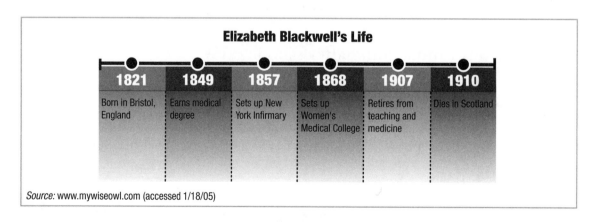

Source: www.mywiseowl.com (accessed 1/18/05)

1. What inference can you make based on what you read?

   Ⓐ Elizabeth was a person who cared about other people.

   Ⓑ Elizabeth was lazy as a child.

   Ⓒ Elizabeth was big for her age.

   Ⓓ Elizabeth was good at everything she did.

2. How was Geneva Medical College different from other medical schools?

   Ⓐ Geneva was bigger than other medical schools.

   Ⓑ Geneva let Elizabeth study medicine there.

   Ⓒ Geneva had other students that were women.

   Ⓓ Geneva was a brand-new medical school.

3. Why did Elizabeth Blackwell want to become a doctor?

   Ⓐ She liked to take care of sick animals.

   Ⓑ She wanted to make a lot of money.

   Ⓒ She wanted to help women with their health problems.

   Ⓓ She wanted to do something no other woman had done.

4. Based on the passage, which statement is true?

   Ⓐ Before Elizabeth went to medical school, anyone could become a doctor.

   Ⓑ Men wanted to become doctors, and women wanted to become nurses.

   Ⓒ Most medical schools and hospitals did not want Elizabeth there.

   Ⓓ Elizabeth cared equally for the health problems of men and women.

GO ON

5. Look at the time line on page 2. What inference can you make?

Ⓐ Elizabeth worked as a doctor for more than 50 years.

Ⓑ Elizabeth received many honors for her work.

Ⓒ Elizabeth helped young men to become doctors.

Ⓓ Elizabeth preferred to live in the United States.

Read this passage. Then answer questions 6–10 by filling in the circle next to the best answer.

The First Day

Tanisha held Roy's hand. She was glad her big brother was there. The door would open soon. It was the first day of school. Roy was starting fourth grade. Tanisha was in second. They were both African-American children who, for the first time, were going to school with white children.

Things had changed. African-American and white children had always gone to separate schools. Now they would go to school together.

Roy and Tanisha looked at the other children. Some had light skin. Some had darker skin. Many were with their parents.

The school door opened. A woman stood there smiling. "Come in, children," she said. The children walked inside. They were very quiet. No one knew where to go.

Roy helped Tanisha find her classroom. Tanisha found an empty seat. Next to her was a girl with blond hair. The girl seemed about to cry. She looked scared. Tanisha was also scared, but she smiled. The blond girl's face changed. She smiled shyly.

Roy stood in the hall. He looked through a glass pane in the door. He thought Tanisha looked brave. Then Tanisha saw Roy. She waved to him.

6. The beginning of the story takes place—

Ⓐ at a computer lab.

Ⓑ inside a classroom.

Ⓒ at a house.

Ⓓ outside a school.

GO ON

7. What happened when the school door opened?

  Ⓐ The children shouted and ran inside.

  Ⓑ A woman smiled and greeted the children.

  Ⓒ The children began to cry.

  Ⓓ The children waited outside.

8. How would you describe the way Roy feels about Tanisha?

  Ⓐ Roy is angry at Tanisha.

  Ⓑ Roy doesn't want Tanisha around.

  Ⓒ Roy cares about Tanisha.

  Ⓓ Roy thinks Tanisha is funny.

9. What can you infer about paragraph five?

  Ⓐ The blond girl doesn't like Tanisha.

  Ⓑ Tanisha is in the wrong class.

  Ⓒ The blond girl is angry.

  Ⓓ Tanisha feels less alone.

10. What is the theme of this story?

  Ⓐ Children have a lot to learn.

  Ⓑ Being someplace new can be fun.

  Ⓒ People should help each other.

  Ⓓ Change is less scary if you are not alone.

Vocabulary/Word Study

Read each question and decide which is the best answer. Fill in the circle next to the answer you have chosen.

11. Tia dislikes the Tigers and would not cheer for them. The opposite of *dislike* is—

Ⓐ put down.

Ⓑ admire.

Ⓒ regard.

Ⓓ make fun of.

12. What is the correct plural form of *inch*?

Ⓐ inches

Ⓑ inchs

Ⓒ inchies

Ⓓ inchss

13. Look at the underlined words. Which one has the correct noun ending?

Ⓐ Some people have lots of hobbeys.

Ⓑ Some people have lots of hobbys.

Ⓒ Some people have lots of hobbies.

Ⓓ Some people have lots of hobbyes.

GO ON

14. A dictionary page has the guide words *desk* and *dew*. Which word would you find on that page?

Ⓐ direct

Ⓑ dentist

Ⓒ detour

Ⓓ decay

15. Which guide words could be on a dictionary page with the word *strange*?

Ⓐ stop/stretch

Ⓑ strict/strong

Ⓒ slip/slow

Ⓓ sweet/swim

16. Which word fits best in both sentences?

I watched the _____ fly above the trees.

My little brother got a _____ for his birthday.

Ⓐ cloud

Ⓑ bat

Ⓒ bee

Ⓓ arrow

17. The police questioned Mr. Mendes, but he was innocent. Which word means the opposite of *innocent*?

Ⓐ friendly

Ⓑ busy

Ⓒ away

Ⓓ guilty

18. Look at the underlined words. Which one has the correct noun ending?

Ⓐ Don't forget to brush your <u>tooths</u>.

Ⓑ Don't forget to brush your <u>teeth</u>.

Ⓒ Don't forget to brush your <u>toothes</u>.

Ⓓ Don't forget to brush your <u>toothies</u>.

19. In a dictionary, which word would be on the page with guide words *brave* and *bribe*?

Ⓐ bread

Ⓑ brass

Ⓒ brown

Ⓓ bring

20. Which word fits best in both sentences?

People in the village get water from a _____.

Arjun played _____, but he lost the game.

Ⓐ tank

Ⓑ cup

Ⓒ hard

Ⓓ well

GO ON

Grammar, Usage, and Mechanics

Read each question and decide which is the best answer. Fill in the circle next to the answer you have chosen.

21. Which is a complete sentence?

Ⓐ A small pond with fish and frogs in it.

Ⓑ The afternoon at a friend's farm.

Ⓒ The animals around the barn.

Ⓓ We picked apples from a tree.

22. Which answer corrects the sentence fragment below?

The meeting at City Hall.

Ⓐ The hall meeting at city.

Ⓑ City Hall at the meeting.

Ⓒ The meeting is at City Hall.

Ⓓ The City Hall meeting.

23. Which word correctly completes the sentence?

Mike and Lori ran _____.

Ⓐ quickly

Ⓑ quicklier

Ⓒ quickiest

Ⓓ quick

24. Choose the sentence with the correct underlined word.

Ⓐ A light flashed <u>bright</u> across the field.

Ⓑ A light flashed <u>brightly</u> across the field.

Ⓒ A light flashed <u>brighter</u> across the field.

Ⓓ A light flashed <u>brightest</u> across the field.

25. Which of these is a sentence fragment?

Ⓐ We waited at the bus stop.

Ⓑ Keyshawn rides the bus to work.

Ⓒ Looking for the number 8 bus.

Ⓓ Two people missed the bus.

26. Which answer corrects the sentence fragment below?

Tied a ribbon around it.

Ⓐ Tied a ribbon around the box.

Ⓑ Tied a bright red ribbon around it.

Ⓒ A gift with a ribbon around it.

Ⓓ The girl tied a ribbon around it.

27. Choose the word that best fits in the sentence.

Mr. Pinsky treats all of his students _____.

Ⓐ fair

Ⓑ fairer

Ⓒ fairly

Ⓓ fairest

 **GO ON**

28. Which of these is a compound sentence?

Ⓐ Marta goes to a museum every Saturday.

Ⓑ She likes art and history best.

Ⓒ Marta looks at paintings and learns about the artists.

Ⓓ She enjoys reading, but she likes watching movies, too.

29. Read these sentences.

The fence is so high.

No one can climb over it.

What is the *best* way to combine these sentences?

Ⓐ The fence is so high that no one can climb over it.

Ⓑ The fence is so high, but no one can climb over it.

Ⓒ No one can climb over the fence that is so high.

Ⓓ No one can climb over it, and the fence is so high.

30. Read these sentences.

In the evening, you can hear owls and coyotes.

You can hear them in the forest.

What is the *best* way to combine these sentences?

Ⓐ In the evening, you can hear owls and coyotes, and you can hear them in the forest.

Ⓑ In the evening, you can hear owls and coyotes in the forest.

Ⓒ In the evening in the forest, you can hear them owls and coyotes.

Ⓓ In the forest, you can hear them in the evening, the owls and coyotes.

Open Response

Go back to the passages on pages 2 and 5 to answer these questions. Write your answers in your own words. Use complete sentences.

---

31. Look at the passage "Leading the Way." How do you think the women she helped felt about Elizabeth Blackwell? Write one or two sentences to explain your answer.

_____

_____

_____

_____

---

32. Look at the story "The First Day." Write one or two sentences that describe how Roy helped Tanisha.

_____

_____

_____

_____

GO ON

Writing

Read the prompt. Write your essay on the lines below. If you need more space, continue writing on separate paper.

Write a personal narrative telling about a time when you did something that made you feel embarrassed.

When you write your personal narrative, remember to
- tell what happened in order,
- include descriptive language and sensory details to make your narrative interesting, and
- use correct grammar, spelling, punctuation, and capitalization.

_____

_____

_____

_____

_____

_____

_____

_____

Progress Monitoring Assessments:
Grade-Level Tests
(Level b)

NAME _____   DATE _____

rSkills® Progress Monitoring Test 1b

DIRECTIONS: This is a reading test. Follow the directions for each part of the test, and choose the best answer to each question.

SAMPLE QUESTIONS

Sample A. Mina was in a hurry to get to school. She grabbed her backpack and ran down the stairs. As she entered the kitchen, she bumped the table and spilled the glass of milk her mother had put out for her.

Mina bumped the table because—

Ⓐ she was in a bad mood.

Ⓑ she wasn't paying attention.

Ⓒ she was in a hurry.

Ⓓ she didn't see her mother.

Sample B. Which verb fits correctly in this sentence?

　　Our cat _____ all the time.

Ⓐ sleeping

Ⓑ sleeps

Ⓒ sleep

Ⓓ sleeped

See p. 292 for scoring.

Go on to the next page to begin the test.

Comprehension

Read this passage. Then answer questions 1–5 by filling in the circle next to the best answer.

Can Fire Be Good for a Forest?

Yellowstone National Park is a beautiful place. Millions of tourists visit the park each year to enjoy the plants, animals, and scenery there. In fact, many consider Yellowstone to be a national treasure.

In 1988, fire nearly destroyed this treasure. Lightning fires burned nearly 800,000 acres, which is more than one-third of Yellowstone's forests. News reports described the event as a disaster. But was it?

Scientists believe that the fire was part of a natural cycle. While there have been many fires in Yellowstone's history, after each one, the park has come back better than before.

During the 1988 fire, people worried about the animals that lived in Yellowstone Park. How could these creatures escape such a terrible fire? The animals were smart. They seemed to know that the fire was a natural event. Most of the large mammals moved ahead of the flames to safe areas. Many small animals and non-flying insects burrowed underground to safety. However, millions of flying insects had no chance to escape.

The fire destroyed forests and grasses, but scientists were amazed at how fast the plant life recovered. When the trees burned, the ground beneath them was exposed to the sun. This helped new plants to grow. Burned trees and grasses turned to ashes, which are a natural fertilizer. Rain and melted snow washed the ash into the soil, so the plants grew more quickly than usual.

Millions of older trees were lost in the 1988 fire, yet their seeds survived. The most common tree in Yellowstone Park is the lodgepole pine. The seeds of this tree are formed in cones with a hard coating. The fire melted the coating, releasing millions of seeds. Luckily, the seeds were almost the same color as the ash on the forest floor. This process helped protect the seeds from hungry birds. The ash enriched the soil, and the seeds grew quickly. Soon young trees replaced the older ones that were lost in the fire.

Moose and elk in Yellowstone Park had a difficult time after the fire. Much of their food supply had burned, so many left the park. It was just a temporary move, however. Within several years, these animals returned. Yellowstone's moose population is much smaller now, but there are more elk than before the fire.

The fire actually helped other animals. Hawks had an easier time finding food after the fire because the small animals they preyed upon had fewer places to hide. Birds that nest in tree holes had more places to call home. Damaged trees became cafeterias for the birds. Beetles and other insects eat damaged trees, and these insects were a rich food supply for many kinds of birds.

After the 1988 fire, even grizzly bears came back stronger than ever. Several bears had been hurt, but within a few years the number of bears increased. Experts believe that the park after the fire was a perfect home for the grizzlies.

The Yellowstone fire helped plants and animals in an important way. It increased diversity. Before the fire, Yellowstone had mostly old pine trees. This was good for some plants and animals, but not for others. After the fire, different kinds of plants were able to grow. This new plant life led to more animal life.

The fire in Yellowstone National Park seemed like a disaster while the flames raged. However, the fire was also nature's way of renewing the park, bringing new plant and animal life.

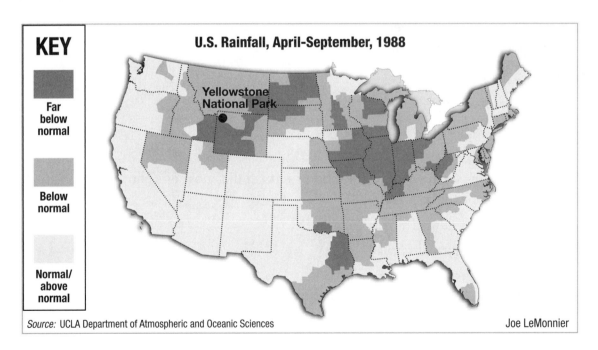

KEY

Far below normal

Below normal

Normal/ above normal

U.S. Rainfall, April–September, 1988

Yellowstone National Park

Source: UCLA Department of Atmospheric and Oceanic Sciences

Joe LeMonnier

GO ON

1. This passage is mostly about—
   Ⓐ a national park's recovery from a fire.
   Ⓑ how forest fires get started.
   Ⓒ why people think Yellowstone is beautiful.
   Ⓓ how trees survive a fire.

2. Which event happened *first*?
   Ⓐ Seeds grew quickly.
   Ⓑ Rain washed ash into soil.
   Ⓒ Trees burned to ash.
   Ⓓ Seeds were released from cones.

3. How did the fire help lodgepole pine trees?
   Ⓐ It released seeds from cones.
   Ⓑ It destroyed insect pests.
   Ⓒ It caused moose to leave the park.
   Ⓓ It created places for birds to nest.

4. Which of these is mentioned *last* in the passage?
   Ⓐ cafeterias for birds
   Ⓑ increased diversity
   Ⓒ moose and elk
   Ⓓ lodgepole pines

5. According to the map, what kind of rainfall did most of Yellowstone
   National Park have in 1988?
   Ⓐ normal rainfall
   Ⓑ below-normal rainfall
   Ⓒ far-below-normal rainfall
   Ⓓ above-normal rainfall

Read this passage. Then answer questions 6–8 by filling in the circle next to the best answer.

A New Life

Lucia, her parents, and her four brothers had been on the boat for more than a week. They had come from a tiny village in Italy.

The family landed in Chester, Pennsylvania. Chester is a town on a river near Philadelphia. Lucia was surprised when the boat traveled up the river. The river was much wider than the ones back home.

It took about half an hour for the boat to approach the dock and tie up. The crew let down the gangway. Lucia's family hurried to their room. They gathered up their suitcases. Papa had their papers. They would need passports for the adults and birth certificates for the children. Without these documents, they could not enter America.

Lucia's bag was heavy. She had brought as many of her belongings as she could. She followed her family as they carried their bags through the ship to the gangway. They walked slowly down the ramp. At the bottom, their feet touched American soil for the first time.

For a moment, no one did anything. They just stood and stared. A sailor hurried them away from the gangway. The family followed the crowd to the immigration office.

Even though she was struggling to keep up, Lucia gazed at her new surroundings. The buildings were very different from those in her village. Some of the houses back home were hundreds of years old, but they were pretty and well kept. These buildings were plain. Lucia's village had trees everywhere, but here there were few trees.

Going through immigration seemed to take forever. Lucia's parents talked to different people in a mix of English and Italian. One man spoke to Lucia. She didn't understand what he said, but she tried her best. A doctor examined each family member. After several hours, an official told the family they were allowed to stay in America.

The family left the immigration building. Outside they searched for Uncle Nico, but he was nowhere to be seen. Papa seemed worried. This trip had been Uncle Nico's idea. He said there was work for everyone.

GO ON

Papa told everyone to sit down. They would wait for Uncle Nico. There was nothing else they could do. Just then, a small truck drove up with its horn honking. Uncle Nico was in the passenger seat. Another man was driving.

Uncle Nico jumped out of the truck and hugged everyone. He told Lucia how pretty she looked. He hugged everyone again. Then he and Papa threw the suitcases into the back of the truck.

Uncle Nico told the children to get into the back of the truck with the luggage. He closed the door behind them. Mama and Papa squeezed into the front seat with the driver. The truck started down the road. Lucia and her family had begun the first day of their new life in America.

6. The boat carrying Lucia's family landed in—

Ⓐ Delaware.

Ⓑ Philadelphia.

Ⓒ Naples.

Ⓓ Chester.

7. What happened right after the boat reached the dock?

Ⓐ The gangway was let down.

Ⓑ The family met with immigration.

Ⓒ The captain shook hands with everyone.

Ⓓ The family stepped onto American soil.

8. When the family reached the bottom of the gangway, they—

Ⓐ waited for hours.

Ⓑ rushed to the immigration building.

Ⓒ met Uncle Nico.

Ⓓ looked around for a moment.

Read this passage. Then answer questions 9 and 10 by filling in the circle next to the best answer.

Finding Work

The two most important tasks for new immigrant families in America are finding work and a place to live. Lucia's family was lucky. Uncle Nico had taken care of things.

After driving less than a mile, the truck stopped in front of a brick building. This was where Uncle Nico lived. The basement apartment was available. The family took their bags from the truck and entered their new home.

Lucia thought the apartment was too small for them. Mama and Papa said it would be fine. The boys didn't know what to think. The apartment had little furniture. Everyone would be sleeping on the floor.

Uncle Nico told Mama to stay with the boys and start unpacking. He hurried Papa and Lucia back to the truck. The driver went just a few blocks. He stopped in front of a factory.

Uncle Nico led Papa and Lucia into the factory building. He introduced them to the boss. The man shook father's hand. He didn't speak Italian, but Uncle Nico interpreted. The man offered Papa a job as a tailor. Papa had been a tailor in Italy, and he was an expert. Through Uncle Nico, the boss offered Lucia a job as a helper. She would make pockets. Papa accepted for her. To Lucia's surprise, the boss wanted them to start work right away.

9. Right after they saw the apartment, Lucia and Papa—
Ⓐ met the boss.
Ⓑ went to work.
Ⓒ got back into the truck.
Ⓓ helped Mama unpack.

10. What kind of work would Lucia do?
Ⓐ cutting cloth
Ⓑ making pockets
Ⓒ driving a truck
Ⓓ working in the office

GO ON

Vocabulary/Word Study

Read each question and decide which is the best answer. Fill in the circle next to the answer you have chosen.

11. If you arrange something more than once, you—

Ⓐ unarrange it.

Ⓑ nonarrange it.

Ⓒ rearrange it.

Ⓓ prearrange it.

12. Choose the word that best completes this sentence.

The deer seemed to vanish, then it simply _____.

Ⓐ reappeared.

Ⓑ unappeared.

Ⓒ preappeared.

Ⓓ exappeared.

13. In which answer is *only* the suffix underlined?

Ⓐ enjoy<u>able</u>

Ⓑ mov<u>able</u>

Ⓒ chang<u>eable</u>

Ⓓ val<u>uable</u>

14. It was unfortunate that Todd hurt his leg the day before the big race. The word *unfortunate* has almost the same meaning as—

Ⓐ cruel.

Ⓑ lucky.

Ⓒ bad.

Ⓓ cold.

15. Everyone seemed to enjoy the music that the band played.
The opposite of *enjoy* is—

Ⓐ like.

Ⓑ remember.

Ⓒ lose.

Ⓓ dislike.

16. It was obvious that someone was home because food was on the table.
Choose the word that is an antonym for *obvious*.

Ⓐ easy

Ⓑ simple

Ⓒ hidden

Ⓓ clear

17. Which word means a "person who directs"?

Ⓐ director

Ⓑ direction

Ⓒ directed

Ⓓ directing

18. Ms. Sanchez will identify one student from each class.
Choose the synonym for *identify*.

Ⓐ mark

Ⓑ remember

Ⓒ allow

Ⓓ select

GO ON

19. After working all night, Mr. Jackson was weary.

What does *weary* mean?

(A) excited

(B) tired

(C) strong

(D) cold

20. We met the builder.

The word *builder* means—

(A) one who builds.

(B) not build.

(C) before building.

(D) build again.

Grammar, Usage, and Mechanics

Read each question and decide which is the best answer. Fill in the circle next to the answer you have chosen.

21. Which of these is a complete sentence?
    - Ⓐ Pieces of glass all over the ground.
    - Ⓑ The worker fixed the window.
    - Ⓒ Wind and a branch against the window.
    - Ⓓ The crash of breaking glass.

22. Which sentence has correct end punctuation?
    - Ⓐ What a wonderful library your school has?
    - Ⓑ Where is my library card?
    - Ⓒ Do you want to go with me.
    - Ⓓ This is my favorite book,

23. Read the sentence and sentence fragment. Which is the best way to correct them?

    The couch is new. And the two chairs.
    - Ⓐ The couch and the two chairs are new.
    - Ⓑ The couch is new and the two chairs.
    - Ⓒ The couch is new with the two chairs.
    - Ⓓ The couch is new. And the two new chairs.

24. Which sentence has correct capitalization?
    - Ⓐ Orcelia used to live in aspen, colorado.
    - Ⓑ Orcelia used to live in aspen, Colorado.
    - Ⓒ orcelia used to live in Aspen, colorado.
    - Ⓓ Orcelia used to live in Aspen, Colorado.

GO ON

25. Which of these is a complete sentence?

    (A) A mall with many stores.

    (B) Shopping for new clothes.

    (C) Pants, blue shirts, and shoes.

    (D) Jorge has a new job.

26. Which sentence should end with a question mark?

    (A) Hundreds of people arrived today

    (B) Do you know who they are

    (C) The people came from China

    (D) What an exciting day it was

27. Read the sentence and sentence fragment. Which is the best way to correct them?

    Olga lives in San Diego. Misses her family.

    (A) Olga lives and misses her family in San Diego.

    (B) Olga lives in San Diego, but she misses her family.

    (C) Olga lives in San Diego or misses her family.

    (D) In San Diego, Olga lives and misses her family.

28. Which sentence uses capital letters correctly?

    (A) Uncle Ray took us to Stone Mountain.

    (B) Uncle Ray took us to stone Mountain.

    (C) Uncle Ray took us to Stone mountain.

    (D) Uncle ray took us to stone mountain.

29. Which is a simple sentence written correctly?

Ⓐ Dinah goes to Yosemite National Park every year.

Ⓑ She and her father and her little brother, Jake.

Ⓒ Dinah enjoys hiking, but she does not like camping.

Ⓓ Too many strange noises at night, and it's dark.

30. Which of these is a compound sentence?

Ⓐ Graham and Charlie are brothers and twins.

Ⓑ They look alike and sound alike.

Ⓒ Graham gets up early, but Charlie sleeps late.

Ⓓ Their last name is Mullen, an Irish name.

GO ON

Open Response

Go back to the passages on pages 2 and 5 to answer these questions. Write your answers in your own words. Use complete sentences.

31. Look at the passage "Can Fire Be Good for a Forest?" Write two or three sentences to describe how the animals reacted to the Yellowstone fire.

_____

_____

_____

_____

_____

32. Look at the story "A New Life." Write two or three sentences about what the family did after the boat reached the dock.

_____

_____

_____

_____

_____

Writing

Read the prompt. Write your essay on the lines below. If you need more space, continue writing on separate paper.

In "A New Life," Lucia looks at her new surroundings in Pennsylvania. Explain what a visitor would see if he or she arrived in *your* city or town for the first time.

When you write your essay, remember to

- state the main topic,
- include details that support the main idea, and
- use correct grammar, spelling, punctuation, and capitalization.

_____

_____

_____

_____

_____

_____

_____

_____

rSkills® Progress Monitoring Test 2b

DIRECTIONS: This is a reading test. Follow the directions for each part of the test, and choose the best answer to each question.

SAMPLE QUESTIONS

Sample A. Choose the sentence with correct end punctuation.

Ⓐ I don't like to eat vegetables?

Ⓑ Did Sara find her jacket.

Ⓒ Which movie should we see.

Ⓓ Do you want to play basketball?

Sample B. Which pair of words is in the same word family?

Ⓐ pen/pencil

Ⓑ fun/funny

Ⓒ forget/forward

Ⓓ dull/doll

See p. 293
for scoring.

Go on to the next page to begin the test.

Comprehension

Read this passage. Then answer questions 1–5 by filling in the circle next to the best answer.

When Cliques Don't Click

Every school has cliques, or groups of kids who hang out together. Members of cliques usually have something in common. They may dress alike, live in the same part of town, or share common interests.

Having a ready-made group of friends at school can be fun. Being in a clique can make a student feel like he or she belongs. However, cliques can also cause problems. Only certain people are allowed to join, while others are rejected. Clique members may refuse to associate with people outside of their circle. What's worse, they may single out one person to pick on. For the person who gets picked on, school can become a terrifying and lonely place.

Some cliques have hazing. Kids who want to join have to do something the clique tells them to do. The hazing may involve foolish pranks, dangerous acts, or even violence. Students can be hurt physically and emotionally. They may even end up in the hospital. Despite these dangers, many kids are willing to do whatever it takes to be accepted.

Being on the "inside" isn't always a great thing, however. Sometimes a clique member secretly disagrees with the clique rules. He or she may want to be friends with someone outside the group or feel pressured to act mean towards someone. A clique often criticizes someone who tries to stand up for what he or she believes.

People usually have roles in cliques. One person is the group leader. The leader tends to be more self-confident than the others. This gives him or her power over the others. Unfortunately, the leader may use his or her power in destructive ways. If the leader dislikes someone, he or she can easily turn the rest of the group against that person, too. Another role is the "sidekick." The sidekick wants to be like the leader, but settles for the role of best friend. A "floater" is often friendly with kids from several groups.

Many schools are taking steps to handle the problems caused by cliques. Some schools offer training for teachers and students. Teachers who go through the training learn to recognize when a clique is getting out of hand. They also learn how to help a student who is victimized by a clique.

Clique members who go through the training learn about how their behavior affects their classmates. The trainer reminds them that they don't have to be in a clique to have close friends. The trainer also encourages non-clique members to be true to themselves and stick to what they believe.

Many students do not belong to cliques. Even when invited, they resist the pressure to join. These students want to think for themselves and choose their own friends.

1. The main idea in this passage is that—
Ⓐ cliques are a good thing.
Ⓑ cliques can be hurtful.
Ⓒ most kids belong to a clique.
Ⓓ hazing should be against the law.

2. Which of these does the passage mention *first*?
Ⓐ Some kids are injured during hazing.
Ⓑ Many students do not belong to a clique.
Ⓒ Floaters are friends with kids from several groups.
Ⓓ Cliques only allow certain people to join.

3. Choose the sentence that best summarizes the third paragraph.
Ⓐ Hazing puts kids in danger.
Ⓑ Hazing can be fun.
Ⓒ Many kids refuse to take part in hazing.
Ⓓ Hazing only happens once a year.

4. Choose the sentence that best summarizes the sixth paragraph.
Ⓐ The "sidekick" is the best friend of the clique leader.
Ⓑ Trainers help students that are not members of a clique.
Ⓒ Many schools try to deal with cliques through teacher and student training.
Ⓓ Parents should talk to their children about belonging to a clique.

5. Choose the sentence that best summarizes the last paragraph.
Ⓐ Only a few students are popular enough to become floaters.
Ⓑ Parents and teachers can help students avoid joining a clique.
Ⓒ Many independent-minded students resist the pressure to join a clique.
Ⓓ Trainers help students to become popular enough to join a clique.

GO ON

Read this passage. Then answer questions 6–10 by filling in the circle next to the best answer.

The Train to Nowhere

"Are you sure you have everything?" Mrs. Johnson asked.

"I think I packed everything I own!" Jeremiah told his mother. "It's time to go." He was anxious to meet his friends Nathaniel and James.

"Be sure to write to let us know that you arrived safely," Jeremiah's dad said gravely.

"I promise," Jeremiah said. He hugged his parents. Then he dashed out the door and down the street, with his suitcase bumping wildly against his legs.

Nathaniel and James were already at the trolley stop when Jeremiah arrived. He was just in time. Moments later, he heard a clanging bell as the trolley car pulled in. The boys climbed aboard. They were headed for the 30th Street train station.

"This sure beats school, doesn't it?" said Nathaniel.

Jeremiah felt a wave of shame. A week ago, he had been expelled for disorderly behavior. Nathaniel and James had quit school soon after that. The country was in the Great Depression, and millions of people were out of work. Many young men were leaving school to help support their families.

Jeremiah and his friends were fortunate. Although barely into their teens, they had found jobs with the Civilian Conservation Corps. The Civilian Conservation Corps was hiring young men at sites around the country. The boys were headed for Arizona, where they would work at Petrified Forest National Park. Their jobs would involve physical labor, but they looked forward to their new life.

The boys hopped off the trolley as it reached the train station, and elbowed their way through the crowd. They were looking for platform 23. There, they checked in with Mr. Carlotti, the head of their work group, and boarded the train.

"Over here!" shouted James. Although the car was nearly full, he had found three seats together. The boys tossed their bags into the overhead rack and sat down. They had a long trip ahead of them.

It took four days to reach their destination. On the way, the train passed through ever-changing cities, towns, and fields. Some of the boys saw mountains and deserts for the first time.

The train had a dining car and restrooms, but there was no place to sleep. At night, Jeremiah used his tattered wool coat as a pillow. There were few complaints, however. For boys from the city, this was an adventure! Besides, Jeremiah couldn't stop thinking about the money he would earn. His job paid $30 a month.

The government would send most of Jeremiah's money home to his family. The Conservation Corps offered free meals and a place to live, so five dollars a month would be more than enough for Jeremiah's needs.

On the fourth day, the train stopped in what appeared to be the loneliest place on earth.

"Welcome to Adamana, boys!" Mr. Carlotti shouted.

Jeremiah gazed out the window and whistled softly under his breath. "This is nowhere, Mr. Carlotti," he said.

Nathaniel and James exchanged glances as they gathered their bags. The three boys jumped down from the train and looked around. Except for a few rundown buildings, the place was almost barren. Mr. Carlotti directed the group to a waiting bus that would carry them on the final part of their journey.

It would be hours before the bus reached Petrified Forest National Park. There, the boys would settle into barracks. Although the ride seemed endless, Jeremiah felt a stir of excitement. There was much to look forward to. His new home offered hot meals and a cot to sleep on. Tomorrow, he would begin his new job. Best of all, he was helping to support his family.

6. Where does the beginning of the story probably take place?

Ⓐ on a train

Ⓑ in a desert

Ⓒ on an airplane

Ⓓ in a city

GO ON

7. Jeremiah was embarrassed because—

(A) he was kicked out of school.

(B) he didn't have a job.

(C) he felt homesick.

(D) he was late for the train.

8. How did the boys get to the train station to begin their journey to Adamana?

(A) They took a busy trolley.

(B) They walked from home.

(C) They were driven by Jeremiah's parents.

(D) They were driven in a Civilian Conservation Corps bus.

9. What made the trip difficult for Jeremiah and his friends?

(A) There was no food or water on the train.

(B) The trip took more than a month.

(C) The boys had to sleep in their seats.

(D) The boys had to stand up for much of the trip.

10. In what time period does the story take place?

(A) during World War II

(B) during the Industrial Revolution

(C) during the Great Depression

(D) during the Gulf War

Vocabulary/Word Study

Read each question and decide which is the best answer. Fill in the circle next to the answer you have chosen.

11. Choose the word that is *not* in the same word family as the others.

Ⓐ newest

Ⓑ newborn

Ⓒ renew

Ⓓ newt

12. Which pair of words are homophones?

Ⓐ juicy/jewelry

Ⓑ stair/stare

Ⓒ guide/glide

Ⓓ except/expect

13. The explorers advanced slowly through the heavy snow.
In this sentence, *advanced* means—

Ⓐ seemed worried.

Ⓑ looked around.

Ⓒ listened carefully.

Ⓓ moved forward.

14. The family left hastily so they wouldn't miss their plane.
In this sentence, *hastily* means—

Ⓐ thoughtfully.

Ⓑ quickly.

Ⓒ slowly.

Ⓓ sadly.

GO ON

15. Which of these words is a compound word?

Ⓐ daylight

Ⓑ problem

Ⓒ necessary

Ⓓ medicine

16. Which word could you combine with *sea* to form a compound word?

Ⓐ swim

Ⓑ sun

Ⓒ weed

Ⓓ wet

17. Choose the word that best fits in the sentence.

Mr. Franklin will be the last _____ at the assembly today.

Ⓐ speaking

Ⓑ speaker

Ⓒ speaks

Ⓓ unspeakable

18. Choose the word that best fits in the sentence.

Janelle bought a new _____ of shoes.

Ⓐ pair

Ⓑ pear

Ⓒ pare

Ⓓ peer

19. Thunder and lightning struck many times during that frightful storm.

In this sentence, *frightful* means—

Ⓐ funny.

Ⓑ quiet.

Ⓒ scary.

Ⓓ boring.

20. Which word can you combine with *time* to form a compound word?

Ⓐ side

Ⓑ watch

Ⓒ hand

Ⓓ table

GO ON

Grammar, Usage, and Mechanics

Read each question and decide which is the best answer. Fill in the circle next to the answer you have chosen.

21. How would you correct this run-on sentence?

The movie was about to start Joan was still buying popcorn.

Ⓐ The movie was about to start, but Joan was still buying popcorn.

Ⓑ The movie was about to start because Joan was still buying popcorn.

Ⓒ The movie, which was about to start. Joan was still buying popcorn.

Ⓓ The movie was about to start. Joan, who was still buying popcorn.

22. Which sentence contains a past-tense verb?

Ⓐ Let's read a book.

Ⓑ She walks to the store every day.

Ⓒ Please help me move this table.

Ⓓ Tanisha played with her cousin.

23. Which sentence has correct word order?

Ⓐ People many waited at the bus stop.

Ⓑ Roy is holding a blue balloon.

Ⓒ Samantha wants to visit her friend best.

Ⓓ This is my brother little.

24. Which sentence shows the correct use of commas?

Ⓐ Our new sofa chair and table were just delivered.

Ⓑ Our new sofa chair, and table were just delivered.

Ⓒ Our new sofa, chair, and, table were just delivered.

Ⓓ Our new sofa, chair, and table were just delivered.

25. What is the best way to correct this run-on sentence?

Papa made a sandwich for me it was a turkey sandwich.

Ⓐ Papa made a turkey sandwich for me.

Ⓑ A turkey sandwich Papa made for me.

Ⓒ Papa made a sandwich for me, but it was a turkey sandwich.

Ⓓ Papa made a turkey sandwich, and he made it for me.

26. In which sentence is the word order correct?

Ⓐ Lina asked the man what he was building.

Ⓑ What Lina asked the man was he building.

Ⓒ Lina asked the man what he building was.

Ⓓ Lina the man asked what building he was.

27. Which sentence uses the correct verb tense?

Ⓐ Yesterday a black dog comes to our door.

Ⓑ I see the same dog at school two days ago.

Ⓒ Mrs. Vanderhorn told the dog to go away.

Ⓓ She loses her own dog last week.

28. In which sentence are commas used correctly?

Ⓐ Mr. Maliki drove through Texas, New Mexico, and, Arizona.

Ⓑ Mr. Maliki drove through Texas, New Mexico, and Arizona.

Ⓒ Mr. Maliki, drove through Texas, New Mexico and Arizona.

Ⓓ Mr. Maliki drove, through Texas, New Mexico, and Arizona.

GO ON

29. Read these sentences.

> On Saturday, our team played two games. We played against the Bobcats.

How can these sentences *best* be joined without changing the meaning?

Ⓐ On Saturday, our team played two games we played against the Bobcats.

Ⓑ On Saturday, we played two games against our team, the Bobcats.

Ⓒ On Saturday, our team played two games against the Bobcats.

Ⓓ On Saturday, our team played two games, and we played against the Bobcats.

30. Read these sentences.

> Hans was so excited about the concert. He waited in line for three hours.

What is the *best* way to combine these sentences?

Ⓐ Hans was so excited about the concert that he waited in line for three hours.

Ⓑ Hans was so excited about the concert, and he waited in line for three hours.

Ⓒ Hans was so excited about the concert, but he waited in line for three hours.

Ⓓ Hans waited in line for three hours and was so excited about the concert.

Open Response

Go back to the passages on pages 2 and 5 to answer these questions. Write your answers in your own words. Use complete sentences.

31. Look at the passage "When Cliques Don't Click." In no more than three sentences, summarize why cliques can be a problem at school.

_____

_____

_____

_____

32. Look at the story "The Train to Nowhere." Describe Adamana, the place where the train stopped, in two to three sentences.

_____

_____

_____

_____

GO ON

Writing

Read the prompt. Write your essay on the lines below. If you need more space, continue writing on separate paper.

You read the story "The Train to Nowhere" (on pages 5 and 6). You may want to read it again. What did you learn from reading this story? Use details from the story to support your answer.

When you write your essay, remember to
- show your understanding of the story,
- give examples from the story, and
- use correct grammar, spelling, punctuation, and capitalization.

_____

_____

_____

_____

_____

_____

_____

_____

_____

rSkills® Progress Monitoring Test 3b

DIRECTIONS: This is a reading test. Follow the directions for each part of the test, and choose the best answer to each question.

SAMPLE QUESTIONS

Sample A. The roads were covered with snow. No one could go anywhere. Mrs. Johnson had to get to the hospital. She was about to have a baby.

The problem in this story is that—

Ⓐ the snow would soon melt.

Ⓑ Mrs. Johnson couldn't get to the hospital.

Ⓒ school was probably closed because of snow.

Ⓓ the hospital was far away.

Sample B. The past tense of *work* is—

Ⓐ works.

Ⓑ working.

Ⓒ worked.

Ⓓ worker.

See p. 294 for scoring.

Go on to the next page to begin the test.

Comprehension

Read this passage. Then answer questions 1–4 by filling in the circle next to the best answer.

Mummies Around the World

Most people who hear the word "mummy" usually think of Egypt. However, mummies have also been found in other parts of the world. In fact, the world's oldest mummies were found in Chile and Peru. These countries are in South America.

The South American mummies are different from Egyptian mummies. The bodies were actually taken apart and dried. Then they were put back together. People who preserved the bodies used sticks and grasses to hold them together. Sometimes they also used animal skins. The mummies were painted, so they all looked alike. Scientists think that these mummies were supposed to stand up.

Scientists have discovered other kinds of mummies in South America. South American tribes probably made these mummies to preserve the remains of human sacrifices. After the victims were killed, their bodies were buried in a sitting position. A mummy's hands were arranged close to the face. Its knees were propped up under the chin. The dry air and cold temperatures preserved the bodies.

Mummies have also been found in Europe. The most famous one was called Otzi the Iceman. In 1991, two hikers found Otzi in Italy near the Austrian border. At first, people didn't realize that Otzi was a mummy. His clothes and tools were in very good condition. They thought he was someone who had died recently. Scientists were surprised to learn that Otzi was about 3,000 years old! The discovery of Otzi helped scientists learn about life during the time that Otzi lived.

In Central Asia, ancient people called Scythians buried their dead in ground that was often frozen. Some of these mummies are close to 3,500 years old. Many have fancy tattoos. Scientists have found these mummies in blocks of ice. The ice preserved the bodies so well that the tattoos can still be seen. Scientists thaw the ice to study the mummies. Once a body is thawed, however, it must be kept in a cold place. Otherwise it will decompose. Many Scythian burial sites have not been dug up yet. Some scientists worry that the increased warming that is taking place around the globe will melt these sites and the mummies will be lost forever.

The British uncovered an unusual kind of mummy. They called it a "bog mummy." Bog mummies are found in swamps or bogs. Chemicals in the bog preserve the bodies. The chemicals also turn the mummies' skin a dark brown color that makes it look like leather. Many bog mummies show signs of injury. Scientists think the people were killed and then thrown into the bog. The killers wanted to hide the bodies. Instead, the bog turned them into mummies!

Mummies have even been found in the United States. In the Southwest, people have come across bodies of Native Americans who were buried long ago. The bodies were covered with rocks to protect them from animals. The hot, dry air helped preserve the bodies.

Otzi the Iceman

6-foot longbow and 14 arrows

Hat made of brown bear fur

Waterproof cape (used as a blanket at night)

Axe with copper head

Stomach remains of deer meat and cereals (Otzi's last meal)

Clothes made of leather and animal fur

Animal-skin shoes stuffed with grass

Source: South Tyrol Museum of Archaeology   Tim Pack

GO ON

1. What problem did South Americans solve using sticks, grasses, and animal skins?

Ⓐ decorating the bodies' faces

Ⓑ bringing bodies back to life

Ⓒ thawing out frozen bodies

Ⓓ putting bodies back together

2. Scientists who find Scythian mummies must be careful because—

Ⓐ the mummies are buried deep in the ground.

Ⓑ the ice blocks are so heavy.

Ⓒ the mummies are buried in a bog.

Ⓓ the mummies decompose when the ice melts.

3. How did the Native Americans protect the bodies of their dead from animals?

Ⓐ They covered the bodies with rocks.

Ⓑ They placed the bodies in tombs.

Ⓒ They threw the bodies in a bog.

Ⓓ They wrapped the bodies in animal skins.

4. Look at the diagram of Otzi the Iceman. Choose the sentence below that best describes Otzi.

Ⓐ Otzi's clothes protected him from the weather.

Ⓑ Otzi had nothing to eat before he died.

Ⓒ Otzi died from an unknown disease.

Ⓓ All of Otzi's clothes were waterproof.

Read this passage. Then answer questions 5–10 by marking the circle next to the best answer.

Shaping Up

Eric looked in the mirror. Standing before him was an out-of-shape boy. He didn't really like what he saw. He also hated that he didn't have any energy and was tired all the time.

"I'm tired of being out of shape," Eric told his mother that night. "What can I do to get muscles?"

"You don't need big muscles," his mother told him. "But you *can* get into shape. All you have to do is eat better and exercise."

Eric knew his mother was right about exercising and changing his diet, but he really didn't want to do either one. Then he remembered how it felt to look in the mirror.

The next morning he had a plan. "What is a healthy breakfast?" Eric asked his mother.

His mom suggested cereal, low-fat milk, and juice. She was busy making Eric's lunch for school. She packed a turkey sandwich on wheat bread with tomato and a Granny Smith apple. This was a change, since Eric usually ate potato chips or cookies for dessert.

At school that day, Eric thought some more about exercise. He decided that going out for a sport would be a good way to get into shape. The swim season was about to start, so Eric talked to the swimming coach. The coach encouraged him to join the team. When Eric told his mother that he had joined the swim team, she was speechless.

For the next two months, Eric was in training. He ate healthy meals, rode his bike every day after school, and sometimes even jogged in the evening. Eric's hard work paid off. His clothes became so loose that he had to buy new ones in a smaller size. He even began to notice muscles in his arms and legs. Best of all, his swimming improved as he lost weight. He was able to swim for longer periods of time.

GO ON

At the first swimming competition, Eric placed first or second in all of his races. He helped the team win the meet. The next day, the principal announced the swim meet results to the entire school over the loudspeaker system. Eric couldn't believe how good he felt when he heard his name. After the announcement, something even better happened. The kids in Eric's class clapped for him and his teammates.

Eric did well in swimming that year. By the end of the season, he was one of the best swimmers on the team. When school ended, he knew exactly how he was going to spend his summer vacation.

Over the summer, Eric rode his bike to the pool every morning. There he practiced with the swim team. The rest of the day, he worked as an assistant teacher at a swim center for young children. When Eric returned home each evening, he ran a mile.

By the end of the summer, Eric was ready for a new challenge. He wanted to compete in a triathlon. In this kind of sports event, he would run and ride a bike, in addition to swimming. Now when Eric looked in the mirror he felt like a completely different person.

5. Where does most of this story take place?

Ⓐ at camp

Ⓑ in the pool

Ⓒ at the ocean

Ⓓ in school

6. Why did Eric want to make changes in his life?

Ⓐ He wanted a summer job.

Ⓑ He wanted to get in shape.

Ⓒ He hoped to surprise his mother.

Ⓓ He didn't like his clothes.

7. Eric's mother was surprised because her son—

Ⓐ no longer looked in the mirror.

Ⓑ stopped eating sweets.

Ⓒ got a summer job.

Ⓓ joined the swim team.

8. Which sentence best describes how Eric felt after his first swim competition?

Ⓐ He decided to join the football team.

Ⓑ He thought he was better than everyone else.

Ⓒ He felt better about himself.

Ⓓ He wanted to quit the swim team.

9. At the end of the story, Eric decides that he is ready for—

Ⓐ new clothes.

Ⓑ a new school.

Ⓒ a new challenge.

Ⓓ a new coach.

10. What is the theme of this story?

Ⓐ Hard work can really pay off.

Ⓑ Everyone should swim.

Ⓒ It is easy to get in shape.

Ⓓ Kids should not tease each other.

GO ON

Vocabulary/Word Study

Read each question and decide which is the best answer. Fill in the circle next to the answer you have chosen.

11. A homophone for *billed* is—

Ⓐ built.

Ⓑ build.

Ⓒ pill.

Ⓓ bill.

12. Which pair of words are homophones?

Ⓐ wing/wind

Ⓑ roar/rare

Ⓒ scene/seen

Ⓓ sled/slide

13. What does the idiom "blow his top" mean in this sentence?

He was so upset at being teased that he was about to *blow his top*.

Ⓐ hurt

Ⓑ angry

Ⓒ tired

Ⓓ messy

14. What does the idiom "drag your feet" mean in this sentence?

Jamal's mother said, "If you *drag your feet*, you will never finish your homework!"

Ⓐ walk without looking

Ⓑ hurt your leg badly

Ⓒ scrape your shoes when you walk

Ⓓ do something slowly

15. Choose the word that is *not* in the same family as the others.

Ⓐ kneel

Ⓑ knowledge

Ⓒ unknown

Ⓓ knows

16. Which word fits best in both sentences?

The _____ decided to change the country's laws.

You'll need a _____ to measure the desk.

Ⓐ yardstick

Ⓑ queen

Ⓒ ruler

Ⓓ president

17. Choose the word that best fits in the sentence.

My broken arm will take two months to _____.

Ⓐ heel

Ⓑ he'll

Ⓒ heal

Ⓓ wheel

18. What does the idiom "in the bag" mean in this sentence?

Derek is worried about winning the game, but I think it's *in the bag*.

Ⓐ a sure thing

Ⓑ too late

Ⓒ a silly game

Ⓓ already lost

GO ON

19. Choose the word that best fits in the sentence.

Isadora learned that she is _____ to the Gomez family.

Ⓐ relation

Ⓑ relative

Ⓒ lately

Ⓓ related

20. Which word fits best in both sentences?

The two teams played a close _____.

This jacket does not _____ my pants.

Ⓐ game

Ⓑ match

Ⓒ suit

Ⓓ contest

Grammar, Usage, and Mechanics

Read each question and decide which is the best answer. Fill in the circle next to the answer you have chosen.

21. Choose the word that fits best in this sentence.

Jen threw the ball and Benn _____ it.

Ⓐ catched

Ⓑ caught

Ⓒ catch

Ⓓ catching

22. Which sentence shows the correct use of commas?

Ⓐ Remember, Shawna, is supposed to bring dessert.

Ⓑ Remember Shawna is supposed to bring, dessert.

Ⓒ Remember Shawna, is supposed, to bring dessert.

Ⓓ Remember, Shawna is supposed to bring dessert.

23. Look at the underlined verb in each sentence. Which sentence is correct?

Ⓐ His favorite team <u>is</u> the Yankees and the Cowboys.

Ⓑ He <u>like</u> team sports more than the others.

Ⓒ My father usually <u>chooses</u> books about sports.

Ⓓ My father and I <u>watches</u> games together.

24. Choose the word that fits best in the sentence.

Our _____ dog likes to visit our house.

Ⓐ neighbor's

Ⓑ neighbors's

Ⓒ neighbor'

Ⓓ neighbors

GO ON

25. Choose the word that fits best in this sentence.

Yesterday, Erik _____ twenty dollars on a book about Egypt.

Ⓐ spend

Ⓑ spent

Ⓒ spended

Ⓓ spends

26. Look at the underlined phrase in each sentence. Which sentence needs a comma after the underlined phrase?

Ⓐ <u>Karin and her friends</u> went to a museum.

Ⓑ <u>The girls</u> learned about mummies and tombs.

Ⓒ <u>In addition</u> they saw some gold jewelry.

Ⓓ <u>One of the rooms</u> had a model of the Nile River.

27. Which sentence is written correctly?

Ⓐ Several players have the talent to win.

Ⓑ Those girls likes to play tennis.

Ⓒ My brother and I practices almost every day.

Ⓓ That girl's teacher are Mr. Jones.

28. Choose the word that fits best in the sentence.

Three _____ parents came to the meeting.

Ⓐ student

Ⓑ student's

Ⓒ students

Ⓓ students'

29. Read this sentence.

> We have missed Ellie a lot _____ she went away to school.

Which word would *best* connect the two parts of this sentence?

Ⓐ or

Ⓑ since

Ⓒ so

Ⓓ but

30. Which sentence is written correctly?

Ⓐ Mateo went to the library so that he could finish his report.

Ⓑ Mateo went to the library; however, he could finish his report.

Ⓒ Mateo went to the library, since he could finish his report.

Ⓓ Mateo went to the library although he could finish his report.

GO ON

Open Response

Go back to the passages on pages 2 and 5 to answer these questions. Write your answers in your own words. Use complete sentences.

31. Look at the passage "Mummies Around the World." Explain why an increase in warm weather around the globe is a problem for scientists who study mummies. Write two or three sentences.

_____

_____

_____

_____

32. Look at the story "Shaping Up." What do you admire most about Eric? Write two or three sentences.

_____

_____

_____

_____

Writing

Read the prompt. Write your essay on the lines below. If you need more space, continue writing on separate paper.

Write an essay to persuade your parent(s) that you should join a team, club, or school group that interests you.

When you write your essay, remember to
- state your opinion,
- give reasons to support your opinion, and
- use correct grammar, spelling, punctuation, and capitalization.

_____

_____

_____

_____

_____

_____

_____

_____

_____

_____

NAME _____ DATE _____

rSkills® Progress Monitoring Test 4b

DIRECTIONS: This is a reading test. Follow the directions for each part of the test, and choose the best answer to each question.

SAMPLE QUESTIONS

Sample A. Dan and Michael stood in front of a dark, old house. "I think it's haunted!" said Dan, backing away. Michael decided to go inside anyway.

In this story, Dan was—

Ⓐ lost.

Ⓑ brave.

Ⓒ weak.

Ⓓ afraid.

Sample B. Which pair of words are homophones?

Ⓐ sing/sang

Ⓑ there/their

Ⓒ race/rice

Ⓓ fun/funny

 See p. 295 for scoring.

Go on to the next page to begin the test.

Comprehension

Read this passage. Then answer questions 1–5 by filling in the circle next to the best answer.

Animal Rescuers

Several groups around the country rescue injured wild animals. Animal doctors and other wildlife experts work for these groups.

When an animal is hurt or sick, people in these groups try to capture it. They are careful not to harm the animal. Sometimes police or rescue workers make the capture. Wildlife officers may help capture bears, mountain lions, and other large animals.

The captured animal is taken to a rescue center. At the center, it gets medical care. If an animal is hurt badly, being treated quickly can save its life.

Even after the animal heals, it still may be unable to live on its own. Some animals need special treatment to make them stronger. This special treatment is called rehabilitation. Rehabilitation can take more than a year. During that time, the animal must find its own food. This stage is very important. An animal that is fed by humans might forget how to survive in the wild.

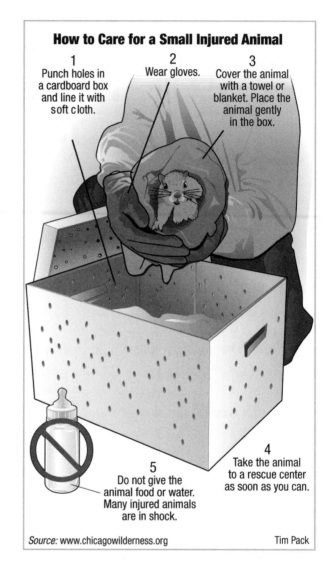

How to Care for a Small Injured Animal

1 Punch holes in a cardboard box and line it with soft cloth.

2 Wear gloves.

3 Cover the animal with a towel or blanket. Place the animal gently in the box.

4 Take the animal to a rescue center as soon as you can.

5 Do not give the animal food or water. Many injured animals are in shock.

Source: www.chicagowilderness.org   Tim Pack

Young animals are kept in a safe area until they are strong. Many must learn how to hunt or hide. Young animals usually learn from adult animals, but these young are not around adults. Instead, they count on human teachers. Imagine if your job were to teach a baby mountain lion how to hunt!

When the animal is strong enough, it is returned to the wild. Workers are careful about when and where they set the animal free. They want the animal to have the best chance to survive. Elk are returned to the mountains in the spring. Mountains are the elk's natural habitat. In springtime, new plants grow. The elk will have plenty of food to eat.

Bears are usually set free in late fall. By that time, their bodies have stored enough fat for the winter. Workers often release a bear near a cave or den. The bear will go into the cave to sleep until spring.

Sometimes an animal is hurt so badly that it can no longer survive on its own. Instead of setting the animal free, workers release it into a protected area. Workers can watch over the animals in this area.

1. When a wild animal is injured, it is more likely to survive if it—

Ⓐ hunts for its own food.

Ⓑ receives medical treatment right away.

Ⓒ returns to the wild as soon as possible.

Ⓓ stays in a protected area.

2. Why must rescue workers sometimes teach young animals how to hunt?

Ⓐ The workers are tired of feeding the animals.

Ⓑ The young refuse to eat what the workers feed them.

Ⓒ The workers like to play with animals.

Ⓓ The young don't have adult animals to teach them.

3. In what way is the release of a rehabilitated elk similar to the release of a rehabilitated bear?

Ⓐ Both elk and bear are released where and when they have the best chance to survive.

Ⓑ Both elk and bear are released in the spring.

Ⓒ Both elk and bear are released in the late fall.

Ⓓ Both elk and bear are released into protected areas.

GO ON

4. Choose the sentence that best summarizes the passage.

Ⓐ Bears hibernate in the winter.

Ⓑ Rescue centers care for injured wild animals.

Ⓒ Young animals must learn how to hunt.

Ⓓ Wild animals can only survive in their natural habitats.

5. According to the diagram on page 2, why should an injured animal not be given food or water?

Ⓐ The blanket the injured animal is wrapped in may get dirty or wet.

Ⓑ Injured animals won't eat from a hand wearing a glove.

Ⓒ Many injured animals are in shock.

Ⓓ Injured animals are too frightened to eat in a rescue center.

Read this passage. Then answer questions 6–10 by filling in the circle next to the best answer.

Eat Right to Play Hard

Eating right is important if you want to succeed at sports. Every athlete needs a healthy diet to play well and win.

When it comes to healthy eating, an athlete follows two main rules. First, it is important to eat a variety of foods. Eating the right foods gives athletes the vitamins and minerals their bodies need to stay healthy. Each kind of food helps the body in a different way. Some foods build muscles. Others boost energy levels. Still other foods help an athlete's body to recover after a workout.

The second rule is to eat the right amounts of food. A person who eats too much will gain weight. Weight gain usually means extra body fat. Extra body fat makes it harder to play most sports. On the other hand, a person who eats too little may not have the energy it takes to play hard. Not eating enough can lead to muscle loss.

There are other eating tips for athletes. One is to eat at the right times. It's important to have a healthy breakfast, a good lunch, and a light dinner at normal meal times. A morning breakfast gives the body fuel for energy. Lunch refuels the body in the middle of the day. Eating a light dinner in the evening makes it less likely that the body will store extra food as fat. It's a good idea to avoid snacking at night, however. Most people use less energy at night, so a late-night snack can lead to weight gain.

Athletes should also time their eating around their sport. A soccer player should eat a large meal about four hours before a big match. Pasta, cereal, and bread are carbohydrates, or energy foods. These foods will boost the player's energy level. High energy allows an athlete to play hard. About an hour before the game, the player should eat a light snack like a banana or a bagel. These are easy to digest.

The soccer player should also eat or drink carbohydrates within an hour after the game. This after-game snack will replace the energy that the body used during the game. Foods like meat, cheese, milk, nuts, or beans are also good to eat after exercise. These foods are high in protein. Protein helps the body to recover after exercise and repairs muscle damage.

GO ON

6. What is one effect of healthy eating that is mentioned in the passage?

Ⓐ gaining too much weight

Ⓑ playing a sport well

Ⓒ losing too much weight

Ⓓ winning all the time

7. Eating too little is a problem for athletes. An athlete who doesn't eat enough will—

Ⓐ gain fat.

Ⓑ lose energy.

Ⓒ lose muscle.

Ⓓ gain muscle.

8. According to the passage, eating too much late at night can lead to—

Ⓐ having more energy.

Ⓑ sleeping too much.

Ⓒ getting a stomachache.

Ⓓ gaining weight.

9. Food for an athlete is most like—

Ⓐ dirt on the ground.

Ⓑ rain from a cloud.

Ⓒ gas for a car.

Ⓓ leaves on a tree.

10. How are meat and other proteins different from carbohydrates like cereal and bread?

Ⓐ Proteins repair muscles while carbohydrates replace energy.

Ⓑ Proteins taste better than carbohydrates.

Ⓒ Proteins use up more energy than carbohydrates.

Ⓓ Proteins are easier than carbohydrates to digest.

GO ON

Vocabulary/Word Study

Read each question and decide which is the best answer. Fill in the circle next to the answer you have chosen.

11. John liked the movie about the legend of the dragon.
A word that means the same as *legend* is—

Ⓐ story.

Ⓑ fact.

Ⓒ map.

Ⓓ lie.

12. Which word fits best in both sentences?

　　Mrs. Gomez is always _____ to us.

　　What _____ of dog is that?

Ⓐ friendly

Ⓑ nice

Ⓒ type

Ⓓ kind

13. Which verb form correctly fits this sentence?

　　The bicycle riders were _____ down the hill.

Ⓐ raceing

Ⓑ race

Ⓒ racing

Ⓓ raced

14. Which underlined verb has the correct ending?

Ⓐ The dog <u>waged</u> its tail.

Ⓑ The dog <u>wagged</u> its tail.

Ⓒ The dog <u>wagedd</u> its tail.

Ⓓ The dog <u>wagded</u> its tail.

15. Look at the words below. Which word has *only* the suffix underlined?

   Ⓐ com<u>fort</u>able

   Ⓑ comfor<u>table</u>

   Ⓒ comfort<u>able</u>

   Ⓓ com<u>fort</u>able

16. Which guide words could be on a dictionary page with the word *steady*?

   Ⓐ search/seem

   Ⓑ stream/stroke

   Ⓒ steep/store

   Ⓓ start/stem

17. Most teenagers require between eight and ten hours of sleep each night. Which word means about the same as *require*?

   Ⓐ try

   Ⓑ enjoy

   Ⓒ dream

   Ⓓ need

18. Which word fits best in both sentences?

   Please _____ the door when you leave.

   Arjun's house is _____ to mine.

   Ⓐ shut

   Ⓑ near

   Ⓒ close

   Ⓓ slam

GO ON

19. Which of these can be combined with the suffix *-ful* to form a real word?

Ⓐ think

Ⓑ clear

Ⓒ success

Ⓓ bright

20. Which word would you find on a dictionary page with the guide words *gone* and *gourd*?

Ⓐ goose

Ⓑ gold

Ⓒ govern

Ⓓ glove

Grammar, Usage, and Mechanics

Read each question and decide which is the best answer. Fill in the circle next to the answer you have chosen.

21. Choose the pronoun that best fits the sentence.

This is Bill's watch. Please give it to _____.

Ⓐ he

Ⓑ him

Ⓒ his

Ⓓ he's

22. How would you correct this sentence?

The movie wasn't no good.

Ⓐ The movie wasn't no good.

Ⓑ The movie wasn't not good.

Ⓒ The movie was not no good.

Ⓓ The movie was not good.

23. Choose the sentence with the underlined words.

Ⓐ The more <u>deeply</u> part of the lake is over there.

Ⓑ The <u>most deepest</u> part of the lake is over there.

Ⓒ The <u>deepest</u> part of the lake is over there.

Ⓓ The <u>more deeper</u> part of the lake is over there.

24. Which sentence uses quotation marks correctly?

Ⓐ "Let's wash the car, suggested Mom.

Ⓑ "Let's wash the car," suggested Mom.

Ⓒ "Let's wash the car, suggested Mom."

Ⓓ "Let's wash" the car, suggested Mom.

GO ON

25. Choose the pronoun that best fits in the sentence.

The ducks swam to the shore. We gave some bread to _____.

Ⓐ us

Ⓑ them

Ⓒ it

Ⓓ they

26. Which sentence is written correctly?

Ⓐ I can hardly see the road.

Ⓑ I can't hardly see the road.

Ⓒ I cannot hardly see the road.

Ⓓ I can hardly not see the road.

27. Choose the word or words that best fit in the sentence.

Dylan is _____ than the other boys in his class.

Ⓐ politer

Ⓑ more polite

Ⓒ politest

Ⓓ most polite

28. Which sentence uses quotation marks correctly?

Ⓐ "Nina asked, Where do you live?"

Ⓑ "Nina asked," Where do you live?

Ⓒ Nina asked, "Where do you live"?

Ⓓ Nina asked, "Where do you live?"

29. Read these two sentences.

> Joel has to baby-sit today. His sister
> Maya cannot be home alone.

Which word could *best* be used to join these sentences?

Ⓐ but

Ⓑ since

Ⓒ or

Ⓓ while

30. What is the correct way to write this sentence?

Marc invited Tina, being my best friend, to the party.

Ⓐ Marc invited Tina to the party, being my best friend.

Ⓑ Marc invited Tina to the party, who is my best friend.

Ⓒ Marc invited Tina, which is my best friend, to the party.

Ⓓ Marc invited Tina, my best friend, to the party.

GO ON

Open Response

Go back to the passages on pages 2 and 5 to answer these questions. Write your answers in your own words. Use complete sentences.

31. Look at the passage "Animal Rescuers." Write two or three sentences that explain how animal rescuers decide when and where to release an animal.

_____

_____

_____

_____

32. Look at the passage "Eat Right to Play Hard." Compare what happens when an athlete eats too much or too little. Write two or three sentences.

_____

_____

_____

_____

Writing

Read the prompt. Write your essay on the lines below. If you need more space, continue writing on separate paper.

Describe your favorite room. The room may be in your home or somewhere else.

When you write your description, remember to
- tell what you are describing,
- use details to make your description interesting, and
- use correct grammar, spelling, punctuation, and capitalization.

_____

_____

_____

_____

_____

_____

_____

_____

_____

rSkills® Progress Monitoring Test 5b

DIRECTIONS: This is a reading test. Follow the directions for each part of the test, and choose the best answer to each question.

SAMPLE QUESTIONS

Sample A. Which word is a synonym for *entire*?

Ⓐ finish

Ⓑ whole

Ⓒ usual

Ⓓ none

Sample B. The barn was old but in good shape. The house was old, too. It was neat and had a nice garden. Horses and cows stood in the field. Juana liked being there.

The setting for this story is—

Ⓐ a farm.

Ⓑ a city.

Ⓒ a forest.

Ⓓ a lake.

See p. 296 for scoring.

Go on to the next page to begin the test.

Comprehension

Read this passage. Then answer questions 1–5 by filling in the circle next to the best answer.

Fighting for Children's Right to Attend School

By 1850, all of the public schools in the state of Massachusetts had both African-American and white students. The city of Boston was different, however. Boston's schools were still separate.

A man named Benjamin Roberts lived in Boston. Roberts wanted his five-year-old daughter, Sarah, to go to school with white children. He tried to send Sarah to four different schools, but they refused to admit her.

Roberts decided to take action. He met with two lawyers named Robert Morris and Charles Sumner. The lawyers sued the Boston school board, and the case went to the state Supreme Court. Benjamin Roberts lost his case, but many people still believed in his cause. They kept fighting for children's right to go to school together. Finally, in 1855, Massachusetts passed a new law that made separate schools for children of different races illegal.

Separate schools also affected children from Native American, Latino, and Asian families. In the 1800s, many of these children were not allowed to attend school with white children in California.

The Tapes had come to California from China. In 1884, the Tapes sent their daughter Mamie to school, but she wasn't admitted.

Like Benjamin Morris, the Tapes filed a lawsuit. The court ruled that Mamie had the same right to enter public school that any other child had. The school officials appealed the case to the state Supreme Court. The state Supreme Court upheld the lower court's decision.

However, the school officials did not give up. They created a separate school for Chinese children and placed Mamie in that school. The officials claimed that the schools were "separate but equal."

Another court case took place in 1945. Felicitas and Gonzalo Mendez's children were not allowed to go to a white school. The Mendez family was Mexican-American. In 1947, Mr. and Mrs. Mendez sued the school district and won. Later that same year, California ended the law that had allowed school segregation. From then on, children of all backgrounds had the right to attend school together.

The Long Fight Against School Segregation

1855	1885	1947	1954	1957	1974
Massachusetts passes the first law prohibiting school segregation.	California State Supreme Court says that public education should be open to all children.	California laws end school segregation for American Indian and Asian children.	Supreme Court declares that separating public school students by race is against the law.	President Eisenhower sends soldiers to escort nine African-American students into a high school in Little Rock, Arkansas.	U.S. District Court orders busing to achieve racial balance in Boston schools.

Source: National Education Association, www.nea.org (accessed 1/19/05)

1. Benjamin Roberts is most like—

Ⓐ someone who leads the way.

Ⓑ a court judge.

Ⓒ a classroom teacher.

Ⓓ a best friend.

2. Why did Mr. and Mrs. Tapes go to court?

Ⓐ Mamie could only go to an Asian school.

Ⓑ Mamie wasn't getting good grades in school.

Ⓒ Their daughter Mamie was not allowed to go to a public school.

Ⓓ Mamie's friends went to a better school than she did.

3. How were Benjamin Roberts's actions similar to those of the Tapes?

Ⓐ Both families fought to send their children to school with white children.

Ⓑ Both families came to the United States from China.

Ⓒ Both families believed in "separate but equal" schools.

Ⓓ Both families lived in California.

GO ON

4. What inference can you make based on what you read in the passage?

Ⓐ California was the only state with separate schools.

Ⓑ Most parents wanted their children to go to separate schools.

Ⓒ Only African-American children were affected by school segregation.

Ⓓ People who fight for their rights can win.

5. Look at the time line on page 3. What inference can you make?

Ⓐ Segregation was abolished quickly.

Ⓑ It takes a long time to win civil rights.

Ⓒ Until 1954, segregation was not an important issue.

Ⓓ African Americans more easily ended segregation than Asian Americans.

Read this passage. Then answer questions 6–10 by filling in the circle next to the best answer.

Kaitlyn's Diary

Friday, November 4, 2005

I just finished my first week at my new school. I feel like I don't belong here. The kids are all city kids. I grew up in a small town. It is so different here. Will I make new friends? My mom tells me not to worry so much. She said that everything would be okay. I hope so. Actually, keeping this diary was my mom's idea. She knows that I like to write.

My family moved to Dawson City last week. My dad has a new job. We used to live in a house with a backyard. Now we live in an apartment. I miss our backyard. I liked to lie on the grass in our yard and watch the clouds in the sky. I also miss my friends Sophie and Tomoko.

There are so many cars here. The streets are filled with them. Before crossing the street, I have to wait until the traffic signal says WALK. Where I used to live, there were fewer cars. My parents used to park our car in the driveway. Now they have to keep it in a parking garage.

My new class is bigger than my old one. There must be 25 kids in it! On my first day, the school principal brought me to my classroom. Everyone stared when I walked into the room. That felt weird. At least the teacher seems nice. Her name is Alison Brown. The children in my class call her Allie. I couldn't believe it! I never called a teacher by her first name before.

During recess, my class goes outside. The girls jump rope. It's different from the way we jumped rope back home. Instead of one rope, they use two. The ropes swing toward each other. Someone told me this is called Double Dutch.

My mom picks me up from school each day. Sometimes we take the bus home. Yesterday I saw a boy from my class on the bus. His name is Jamal. He was with his mother, too. Jamal is nice. He smiled and said hello. Then our moms started to talk. Jamal's family lives in my neighborhood. Jamal and his mom got off the bus one stop before we did.

GO ON

Art class is my favorite. A special teacher comes to our classroom to teach art twice a week. Right now, we are making puppets. The puppet heads are papier-mâché. We will make the puppet bodies out of colored fabric.

My puppet is a girl. She has dark brown hair and brown eyes just like me. I am going to make her a pair of glasses. Then she will *really* look like me! In fact, I'm even going to make my girl puppet a tennis player, just like me. I can make her a tennis racket with cardboard and string. Jamal is making a dinosaur puppet. He said it's a Tyrannosaurus Rex. I think it looks more like an alien from outer space.

6. Based on what you read in her diary, how would you describe Kaitlyn?

Ⓐ She has a good sense of humor.

Ⓑ She likes the city better than the country.

Ⓒ She is excited about making new friends.

Ⓓ She is very serious about everything.

7. Choose the sentence that best describes where Kaitlyn now lives.

Ⓐ Kaitlyn lives in a cabin near the mountains.

Ⓑ Kaitlyn lives in a house in a small town.

Ⓒ Kaitlyn lives in an apartment in a big city.

Ⓓ Kaitlyn lives in a house by the ocean.

8. The last thing Kaitlyn describes is—

Ⓐ her art project.

Ⓑ her school.

Ⓒ her father's new job.

Ⓓ her friend Jamal.

9. What is probably Kaitlyn's favorite sport?

Ⓐ tennis

Ⓑ softball

Ⓒ jump rope

Ⓓ dodgeball

10. What is the theme of this passage?

Ⓐ It is important to have something to believe in.

Ⓑ A lot can change when you move to a new place.

Ⓒ A city is the best place to live.

Ⓓ Diaries are a good way to express yourself.

GO ON

Vocabulary/Word Study

Read each question and decide which is the best answer. Fill in the circle next to the answer you have chosen.

11. The water in the puddle was shallow, so Yoko's feet did not get wet. The opposite of *shallow* is—

Ⓐ deep.

Ⓑ wet.

Ⓒ cool.

Ⓓ neat.

12. What is the correct plural form of *actress*?

Ⓐ actres

Ⓑ actresses

Ⓒ actresss

Ⓓ actreses

13. Look at the underlined words. Which one has the correct noun ending?

Ⓐ We saw mummyes at the museum.

Ⓑ We saw mummys at the museum.

Ⓒ We saw mummies at the museum.

Ⓓ We saw mummeys at the museum.

14. A dictionary page has these guide words: *band/batch*. Which word would you find on that page?

Ⓐ barn

Ⓑ best

Ⓒ bake

Ⓓ ball

15. Which guide words could be on a dictionary page with the word *gate*?

Ⓐ gear/get

Ⓑ gaze/gear

Ⓒ gain/game

Ⓓ garden/gave

16. Which word fits best in both sentences?

Every house on our _____ has a garden.

This _____ of wood is very heavy.

Ⓐ piece

Ⓑ block

Ⓒ street

Ⓓ road

17. Fresh vegetables are plentiful during this time of year.

Which word means the opposite of *plentiful*?

Ⓐ scarce

Ⓑ narrow

Ⓒ tasty

Ⓓ cheap

18. Look at the underlined words. Which one has the correct noun ending?

Ⓐ There were two <u>mouses</u> in our kitchen.

Ⓑ There were two <u>mousies</u> in our kitchen.

Ⓒ There were two <u>mice</u> in our kitchen.

Ⓓ There were two <u>mices</u> in our kitchen.

GO ON

19. Which guide words could be on a dictionary page with the word *hero*?

Ⓐ heart/hedge

Ⓑ heel/help

Ⓒ hew/hide

Ⓓ hen/hesitate

20. Which word fits best in both sentences?

Danny had to fix the _____ on his bike.

Those dogs are running fast, but they will _____ soon.

Ⓐ wheel

Ⓑ tire

Ⓒ slow

Ⓓ chain

Grammar, Usage, and Mechanics

Read each question and decide which is the best answer. Fill in the circle next to the answer you have chosen.

21. Which of the following is a complete sentence?

   Ⓐ Our vacation lasted two weeks.

   Ⓑ Drove to the mountains in Utah.

   Ⓒ Trees around a beautiful lake.

   Ⓓ Camping in tents each night.

22. Which answer corrects the sentence fragment below?

   Went to the zoo with my parents.

   Ⓐ To the zoo with my parents to see to the animals.

   Ⓑ Went to the zoo with my parents to see the animals.

   Ⓒ With my parents to the zoo my friends and I.

   Ⓓ My friends and I went to the zoo with my parents.

23. Which word fits best in this sentence?

   He _____ built the tree house out of branches and boards.

   Ⓐ skillful

   Ⓑ skillfully

   Ⓒ skilled

   Ⓓ skills

24. Choose the sentence with the correct underlined word.

   Ⓐ The new high school is <u>nearest</u> finished.

   Ⓑ The new high school is <u>near</u> finished.

   Ⓒ The new high school is <u>nearly</u> finished.

   Ⓓ The new high school is <u>nearer</u> finished.

GO ON

25. Which of these is a sentence fragment?

Ⓐ Went to the beach this morning.

Ⓑ Geraldo and I looked for shells.

Ⓒ He found a horseshoe crab.

Ⓓ A boy said hello.

26. Which answer corrects the sentence fragment below?

Two boys on our soccer team.

Ⓐ Two boys on our soccer team named Ray and Eduardo.

Ⓑ Two boys who are on our soccer team.

Ⓒ Our soccer team and two boys on it.

Ⓓ Two boys on our soccer team scored goals.

27. Choose the word that best fits in the sentence.

Miranda stood up and walked _____ to the stage.

Ⓐ proud

Ⓑ proudly

Ⓒ prouder

Ⓓ proudest

28. Which of these is a compound sentence?

Ⓐ Jeff eats cereal for breakfast.

Ⓑ He also likes toast and fruit.

Ⓒ My brother is tall, but I am short.

Ⓓ Mom and Dad make scrambled eggs.

29. Read these sentences.

> Ms. Chen is a very good dancer.
> Ms. Chen teaches ballet.

What is the *best* way to combine these sentences?

Ⓐ Ms. Chen teaches ballet, a very good dancer.

Ⓑ Ms. Chen, a very good dancer, teaches ballet.

Ⓒ Teaching ballet, Ms. Chen is a very good dancer.

Ⓓ Ms. Chen is a very good dancer, and she teaches ballet.

30. Read these sentences.

> At the airport, all flights were delayed.
> The flights were delayed because of a storm.

What is the *best* way to combine these sentences?

Ⓐ At the airport, all flights were delayed because of a storm.

Ⓑ All flights were delayed because of a storm at the airport.

Ⓒ Because all flights were delayed, there was a storm at the airport.

Ⓓ At the airport, a storm was delayed because of all the flights.

GO ON

Open Response

Go back to the passages on pages 2 and 5 to answer these questions. Write your answers in your own words. Use complete sentences.

31. Look at the passage "Fighting for Children's Right to Attend School." Describe how Benjamin Roberts felt about the schools that white children went to. Explain your answer in two or three sentences.

_____

_____

_____

_____

32. Look at the story "Kaitlyn's Diary." Write two or three sentences that describe how Kaitlyn's mood changes from the beginning to the end of her diary entry.

_____

_____

_____

_____

Writing

Read the prompt. Write your essay on the lines below. If you need more space, continue writing on separate paper.

Write a personal narrative telling about a time when you did something you had never done before.

When you write your personal narrative, remember to
- tell what happened in order,
- include descriptive language and sensory details to make your narrative interesting, and
- use correct grammar, spelling, punctuation, and capitalization.

_____

_____

_____

_____

_____

_____

_____

_____

_____

rSkills Summative Assessments (Levels a and b)

NAME _____ DATE _____

rSkills® Midyear Test (Level a)

DIRECTIONS: This is a test of reading, writing, and listening. Follow the directions for each part of the test, and choose the best answer to each question.

SAMPLE QUESTIONS

Tari grew up in Mumbai. That is one of the largest cities in India. She moved to the United States with her family. Now she lives in Los Angeles.

Sample A. Tari grew up in—

Ⓐ India.

Ⓑ Mexico.

Ⓒ China.

Ⓓ the United States.

Sample B. Which word means the same as *largest*?

Ⓐ nearest   Ⓒ smallest

Ⓑ biggest   Ⓓ oldest

See p. 297 for scoring.

Go on to the next page to begin the test.

Comprehension

Read this passage. Then answer questions 1–4 by filling in the circle next to the best answer.

Fire in the Night

Tula opened her bedroom window. It was a warm spring night. Even from the sixth floor of her building, she could smell the cherry blossoms. "That's the best smell in the whole world," Tula decided as she fell asleep.

Some time later, Tula woke. She smelled smoke. She heard a fire alarm. Just then, Mama rushed into Tula's room.

"The building is on fire!" Mama cried. "We have to get out now!"

Tula leaped out of bed and put on her slippers. Then she followed Mama out the door to the fire escape. As they hurried down the steps, fire engines arrived. Firefighters ran into the building.

The parking lot quickly filled with residents. They were frightened and confused. Some of them just stood and stared at the fire.

Within an hour, the fire was almost out. But the building was badly damaged. Tula and Mama wondered what was going to happen to them.

Emergency workers passed out blankets and warm drinks. "We are setting up a shelter at the community center," the workers explained. "You will have meals and clothing. You will have a place to sleep. We will help you find new homes."

Mama wrapped a blanket around Tula. "We're going to have a bumpy road ahead of us for a while," Mama began. "But we'll get through it."

Tula nodded. Then she walked over to the cherry trees. She breathed in the sweet scent until the smell of smoke faded away.

1. Where is Tula at the beginning of this story?

Ⓐ in her apartment

Ⓑ in a parking lot

Ⓒ at a fire station

Ⓓ at the community center

2. What happened just before Mama rushed into Tula's room?

Ⓐ Tula opened her bedroom window.

Ⓑ Firefighters ran into the building.

Ⓒ Tula smelled smoke and heard a fire alarm.

Ⓓ Emergency workers passed out blankets.

3. As they hurried out of their apartment, how did Tula and Mama probably feel?

Ⓐ calm

Ⓑ scared

Ⓒ hopeful

Ⓓ proud

4. What happened because of the fire?

Ⓐ Many residents were badly hurt.

Ⓑ The cherry trees burned down.

Ⓒ The residents had no place to live.

Ⓓ Some fire engines were damaged.

GO ON

Read this passage. Then answer questions 5–8 by filling in the circle next to the best answer.

Dodo Birds

Have you ever heard of dodo birds? They became extinct more than 300 years ago.

The dodo was an unusual bird. It was about twice the size of a turkey. It had wings but could not fly. It was mostly gray with short, yellow legs and a long, crooked beak. The dodo used its beak to catch and eat fish. It was also known for its habit of eating stones. The stones may have helped the dodo digest food.

The dodo was native to only one place in the world. It lived on the island of Mauritius in the Indian Ocean. Sailors from Portugal first landed there around 1505. They thought the dodo was a seabird at first. But it actually lived in the forest.

Sailors thought the dodo was amusing. It ate stones and was very clumsy. When it tried to run, its belly dragged along the ground. Some sailors wrote descriptions and drew pictures of dodos. Sometimes they trapped the birds. Then they took them back to Europe in cages. They also hunted and killed many dodos for food.

In 1644, Dutch sailors landed on Mauritius. They brought dogs, pigs, rats, and monkeys with them. These animals had never lived on the island before. The dodo had no defense against them. They attacked the dodos. They ate the dodo's eggs and its young. Before long, the effects of both humans and animals killed off the rest of the dodos. By 1681, all of them were gone.

5. What is this passage mostly about?

   Ⓐ an island in the Indian Ocean

   Ⓑ sailors from Portugal

   Ⓒ forests on the island of Mauritius

   Ⓓ the end of the dodo bird

6. What was unusual about the dodo bird?

   Ⓐ It had wings and a hooked beak.

   Ⓑ It could not fly and sometimes ate stones.

   Ⓒ It was mostly gray with yellow legs.

   Ⓓ It lived in the forest.

7. How did Dutch sailors cause a problem for dodos?

   Ⓐ They thought the dodos were amusing.

   Ⓑ They brought animals that attacked the dodos.

   Ⓒ They wrote descriptions of the dodos.

   Ⓓ They took the dodos back to Europe in cages.

8. Which sentence best summarizes this passage?

   Ⓐ The dodo bird became extinct more than 300 years ago.

   Ⓑ The island of Mauritius is located in the Indian Ocean.

   Ⓒ Sailors first saw dodo birds on the island of Mauritius.

   Ⓓ Dogs, pigs, rats, and monkeys ate the dodo birds' eggs.

GO ON

Read this passage. Then answer questions 9–14 by filling in the circle
next to the best answer.

The Long Ride Home

"Quick, she's coming! Don't let her sit up here!"

As Rosa climbed up the steps, whispers flew through the front
of the bus. Empty seats were suddenly filled. Rosa pretended not
to notice. She found a seat toward the back. From there, she heard
the other kids snicker.

It was like this every afternoon. By now, Rosa was used to it. But
it still hurt. She kept telling herself that middle school would end
someday.

Still, there was a problem. Rosa's stop was one of the last on the bus
route. When she sat in the back, the long, winding drive up the canyon
made her stomach feel queasy. Every afternoon when she got home,
Rosa had to lie down until her insides felt steady again. Sometimes that
took an hour.

When the bus reached Rosa's stop, she walked toward the front.
Mr. Domingo watched her in the mirror. He stopped Rosa by
the steps.

"Young lady," he said, "every day you get off the bus. You look
like you just rode a roller coaster. And I notice that you can't get a seat
up front."

Rosa nodded.

"Well, starting tomorrow, you'll sit in the seat behind me. I'll make
sure of that. How does that sound to you?"

"That sounds fine, Mr. Domingo," Rosa replied. As she climbed off
the bus, she turned and waved. Rosa felt glad to have a new friend.

9. Where does this story take place?

Ⓐ at Rosa's school

Ⓑ on a school bus

Ⓒ at Rosa's house

Ⓓ in a car

10. What is Rosa's main problem in this story?

Ⓐ Some girls at school don't say hello to her.

Ⓑ The bus is so crowded that she never gets a seat.

Ⓒ Riding in the back of the bus makes her feel sick.

Ⓓ She never gets home on time.

11. What happens just after Rosa gets home each day?

Ⓐ She lies down until she feels better.

Ⓑ She does her homework.

Ⓒ She talks to her friends on the phone.

Ⓓ She hears the other kids snicker.

12. How does Mr. Domingo try to help Rosa?

Ⓐ He drives the bus as slowly as he can.

Ⓑ He watches her walk to the front.

Ⓒ He says hello when he sees her.

Ⓓ He gives her a seat at the front.

GO ON

13. At the end of the story, Rosa probably feels—

Ⓐ grateful.

Ⓑ lonely.

Ⓒ worried.

Ⓓ excited.

14. What can you tell about Mr. Domingo from reading this story?

Ⓐ He always minds his own business.

Ⓑ He can be stubborn and impatient.

Ⓒ He reaches out to people who need help.

Ⓓ He has a great sense of humor.

Read this passage. Then answer questions 15–20 by filling in the circle next to the best answer.

A Doctor and a Champion

Sammy Lee was born in Fresno, California, in 1920. His parents came from Korea. They were hopeful about living in the United States.

A Boy With Two Goals

In 1932, the Olympic Games took place in Los Angeles, not far from Sammy's home. Sammy loved the excitement. He decided to become an Olympic diving champion someday.

Sammy knew he should practice all the time. But the local pool was open to nonwhites only one day a week. Sammy could not improve his diving with so little practice. Also, Sammy's father wanted him to become a doctor. For that, Sammy needed excellent grades. Mr. Lee urged Sammy to dive less and study more.

Sammy wanted to please his father. But he made time for diving, too. Sammy became the top student in his high school class. Then he went to college and medical school. All the while, he kept diving and did well.

Years of Hard Work Rewarded

By 1946, Sammy was a doctor and had little time for diving. But he wanted to compete in the 1948 Olympics. So he took time off from work to train. At age 28, he made the U.S. diving team. Then he won two medals in the 1948 Olympics, a bronze and a gold.

GO ON

Four years later, Sammy entered the Olympics again and won another gold medal. Soon afterward, he was named the best amateur athlete in the United States.

Unfortunately, Sammy Lee's father died in 1943. He never saw Sammy become a doctor or an Olympic champion. But he would have been proud.

15. Which is the best summary of this passage?

Ⓐ Sammy Lee became a doctor and an Olympic diving champion.

Ⓑ The rules at Sammy's local pool did not allow him to dive every day.

Ⓒ Sammy Lee watched the Olympics and then made the U.S. diving team.

Ⓓ Mr. Lee wanted Sammy to study more and spend less time diving.

16. Which of these events happened *first*?

Ⓐ Sammy became the top student in his high school class.

Ⓑ Sammy's parents came to the United States from Korea.

Ⓒ Sammy was named the best amateur athlete in the United States.

Ⓓ Sammy won an Olympic gold medal and a bronze medal.

17. Sammy Lee decided to become a champion diver when he—

    Ⓐ arrived in the United States.

    Ⓑ started swimming in the local pool.

    Ⓒ went to medical school.

    Ⓓ watched the Olympics in Los Angeles.

18. Sammy Lee's father most wanted him to—

    Ⓐ improve his diving.

    Ⓑ live in the United States.

    Ⓒ make the Olympic team.

    Ⓓ become a doctor.

19. Which of these events happened *last*?

    Ⓐ Sammy went to medical school and became a doctor.

    Ⓑ Sammy's father died.

    Ⓒ Sammy competed in his second Olympics.

    Ⓓ Sammy watched the 1932 Olympics.

20. Which sentence best summarizes Sammy Lee's diving career?

    Ⓐ He won gold medals in both the 1948 and 1952 Olympics.

    Ⓑ After Sammy won his first Olympic gold medal, he wanted to win another.

    Ⓒ He became a doctor and the best amateur athlete in the United States.

    Ⓓ Sammy trained hard for the Olympics and was proud of reaching his goal.

GO ON

Vocabulary/Word Study

Read each question and decide which is the best answer. Fill in the circle next to the answer you choose.

21. Tula leaped out of bed and put on her slippers.

Which word is a synonym for *leaped*?

Ⓐ yelled   Ⓒ looked

Ⓑ fell   Ⓓ jumped

22. Mama said, "We're going to have a bumpy road ahead of us."

What does the idiom "have a bumpy road ahead" mean?

Ⓐ take a long trip   Ⓒ move to a hilly place

Ⓑ have some problems   Ⓓ buy a new car

23. A few years ago, scientists rediscovered the dodo.

What does *rediscovered* mean in this sentence?

Ⓐ discovered before   Ⓒ discovered again

Ⓑ able to discover   Ⓓ not discovered

24. The bus drove up the long, winding road.

Which word is an antonym for *winding*?

Ⓐ straight   Ⓒ narrow

Ⓑ steep   Ⓓ rocky

25. Mr. Lee went to inquire about the job, but the office was closed.

In this sentence, *inquire* means—

Ⓐ start.   Ⓒ drive.

Ⓑ pay.   Ⓓ ask.

26. In which sentence is *their* used correctly?

Ⓐ The students are working on their projects.

Ⓑ You can hang your raincoat over their.

Ⓒ My friends aren't here yet, but their coming.

Ⓓ Their is someone knocking at our door.

27. In which sentence is *buy* used correctly?

Ⓐ You must be at the train station buy noon.

Ⓑ Where did you buy those sneakers?

Ⓒ We drove buy your old house yesterday.

Ⓓ Everyone must play buy the rules.

28. Camille's dishonesty really bothers me.

Which of these words is in the same word family as *dishonesty*?

Ⓐ dishes

Ⓒ honestly

Ⓑ someone

Ⓓ bothers

29. The teacher collected our homework at the beginning of class.

Which word in the sentence is a compound word?

Ⓐ teacher

Ⓒ homework

Ⓑ collected

Ⓓ beginning

30. Jessie was a survivor of the flood.

The word *survivor* means—

Ⓐ a person who survives.

Ⓒ able to survive.

Ⓑ survive again.

Ⓓ not survive.

GO ON

Grammar, Usage, and Mechanics

The following is a rough draft of a student's story. It contains errors. Read the draft. Then read each question and decide which is the best answer. Fill in the circle next to the answer you choose.

Finding a Memory

(1) My family came to America when I was just four years old. (2) My older brother Igor remembers a lot about our life in Russia. (3) He tells stories about our apartment building. (4) He remembers visiting our grandmother. (5) He can describe our bedroom I don't even remember sharing a room with him!

(6) My sister Katerina remembers things, too. (7) She remembers crossing the <u>neva river</u> in the winter. (8) Very worried about the poor, cold ducks on the ice.

(9) I was jealous of my brother and sister. (10) They had something I did not. (11) At school here in America, my classmates told stories of growing up in other countries. (12) I wanted to share some memories of Russia, but I didn't have any.

(13) Then one day I was doing a science project. (14) I needed two small containers for growing seeds. (15) "Where are those little blue bowls with the stars on them?" I asked my mother.

(16) "Oleg," she laughed, "we <u>leaved</u> those behind in Russia! (17) But you remembered them. (18) You have your own memory of Russia after all!"

31. Which of these is a sentence fragment?

    Ⓐ My family came to America when I was just four years old.

    Ⓑ Very worried about the poor, cold ducks on the ice.

    Ⓒ I needed two small containers for growing seeds.

    Ⓓ She was right.

32. How should sentence 5 be written correctly?

Ⓐ He can describe our bedroom, I don't even remember sharing a room with him!

Ⓑ He can describe our bedroom, or I don't even remember sharing a room with him!

Ⓒ He can describe our bedroom, but I don't even remember sharing a room with him!

Ⓓ He can describe, our bedroom I don't even remember sharing a room with him!

33. Which is the correct way to capitalize the underlined words in sentence 7?

Ⓐ Neva river   Ⓒ neva River

Ⓑ Neva River   Ⓓ Leave as is.

34. Which is the best way to combine sentences 9 and 10?

Ⓐ I was jealous of my brother and sister so they had something I did not.

Ⓑ I was jealous of my brother and sister, they had something I did not.

Ⓒ I was jealous of my brother and sister because they had something I did not.

Ⓓ I was jealous of my brother and sister, or they had something I did not.

35. What is the correct way to write the underlined word in sentence 16?

Ⓐ left   Ⓒ leaving

Ⓑ leave   Ⓓ Leave as is.

GO ON

The following is a rough draft of a student's report. It contains errors. Read the draft. Then read each question and decide which is the best answer. Fill in the circle next to the answer you choose.

The Roosevelts

(1) During the Depression, many Americans lost their jobs. (2) They needed help from leaders who cared about their problems.

(3) Luckily, President Franklin Delano Roosevelt and his wife Eleanor were strong and caring leaders. (4) Both were born into rich, powerful families. (5) However both of them understood the suffering of others.

(6) Eleanor was a shy little girl. (7) Her mother often made fun of Eleanor for being too serious.

(8) Franklin was a young man popular. (9) He had a very easy life until he was 39 years old. (10) Franklin became sick with a disease called polio. (11) Had trouble walking for the rest of his life.

(12) The Roosevelts never gave up. (13) When the Depression hit, they encouraged others not to give up either.

(14) President Roosevelt started many new government programs. (15) Most of these programs helped workers. (16) Eleanor Roosevelt traveled constantly to make sure the programs were helping.

36. What is the correct way to punctuate the underlined part of sentence 5?

Ⓐ However, both of them

Ⓑ However both, of them

Ⓒ However both of them,

Ⓓ However, both, of them

37. How can sentences 6 and 7 *best* be combined?

Ⓐ Eleanor was a shy little girl with her mother often making fun of her for being too serious.

Ⓑ Eleanor was a shy little girl whose mother often made fun of her for being too serious.

Ⓒ Eleanor was a shy little girl, since her mother often made fun of her for being too serious.

Ⓓ Eleanor was a shy little girl, her mother often making fun of her for being too serious.

38. How can sentence 8 best be written?

Ⓐ Franklin was a popular young man.

Ⓑ Popular Franklin was a young man.

Ⓒ Franklin was a young popular man.

Ⓓ Leave as is.

39. Line 11 is a sentence fragment. Which is the best way to correct it?

Ⓐ Trouble walking for the rest of his life.

Ⓑ Having trouble walking for the rest of his life.

Ⓒ He had trouble walking for the rest of his life.

Ⓓ Walking with trouble for the rest of his life.

40. What is the correct way to write the underlined word in sentence 16?

Ⓐ traveling

Ⓑ travels

Ⓒ travel

Ⓓ Leave as is.

Writing

Read the prompt. Write your essay on the lines below and on the next page, or on the answer document.

Think about the last trip you took. Explain where you went and why you took the trip.

When you write your essay, remember to
- state the main topic,
- include details that support the main idea, and
- use correct grammar, spelling, punctuation, and capitalization.

_____

_____

_____

_____

_____

_____

_____

_____

_____

_____

GO ON

Listening

Listen to each passage as your teacher reads it aloud. Then listen to the questions. Choose the best answer to each question. Fill in the circle beside the answer you choose.

41. Ⓐ The principal makes an announcement.

Ⓑ The buses arrive at school.

Ⓒ Will talks to Connie and Jim.

Ⓓ Ms. Baker looks out the window.

42. Ⓐ surprised and afraid

Ⓑ annoyed and impatient

Ⓒ excited and happy

Ⓓ curious and amazed

43. Ⓐ He ignores his friends.

Ⓑ He argues with his friends.

Ⓒ He tries to make his friends feel better.

Ⓓ He amuses his friends to make them laugh.

44. Ⓐ They are anxious to get out of school.

Ⓑ They can't hear the tornado.

Ⓒ They are worried about their parents' safety.

Ⓓ They don't like being farmers' kids.

45. Ⓐ in a classroom

Ⓑ in a cornfield

Ⓒ in a school bus

Ⓓ in a school gym

46. Ⓐ Egyptian farmers

Ⓑ the desert

Ⓒ cat mummies

Ⓓ linen cloth

47. Ⓐ A farmer found an old pet cemetery.

Ⓑ Cat mummies were sent to a museum.

Ⓒ Tourists went to visit Beni Hasan.

Ⓓ People in Egypt mummified their pets.

48. Ⓐ They feared cats.

Ⓑ They loved cats.

Ⓒ They thought cats were strange.

Ⓓ They felt sad about cats.

49. Ⓐ They were treated with respect.

Ⓑ They were placed in a museum.

Ⓒ They were burned in a fire.

Ⓓ They were sold or thrown away.

50. Ⓐ A farmer found an ancient pet cemetery in Egypt.

Ⓑ Mummified cats were wrapped in white linen.

Ⓒ Each of the cat mummies was given a cat mask.

Ⓓ Thousands of pets were buried near Beni Hasan.

NAME _____ DATE _____

rSkills® End-of-Year Test (Level a)

DIRECTIONS: This is a test of reading, writing, and listening. Follow the directions for each part of the test, and choose the best answer to each question.

SAMPLE QUESTIONS

A kiwi is a sweet, juicy fruit. This fruit is light green with small, black seeds. It grows on a vine, and it has a rough, fuzzy skin. Most of the kiwis sold in the United States come from New Zealand.

Sample A. Where do most kiwis come from?

Ⓐ Japan   Ⓒ China

Ⓑ New Zealand   Ⓓ United States

Sample B. It has a rough, fuzzy skin.
Which word means the opposite of *rough*?

Ⓐ hard   Ⓒ hairy

Ⓑ green   Ⓓ smooth

See p. 298 for scoring.

Go on to the next page to begin the test.

Comprehension

Read this passage. Then answer questions 1–4 by filling in the circle next to the best answer.

The Test: A Story From Cambodia

A long time ago, a young man asked to marry a rich man's daughter. But the young man had no money and little to offer. The father had once been poor like the young man. So he decided to give him a chance.

He said, "You may marry her if you can pass a test. For two days, you must stand in cold lake water. You cannot move to warm yourself. If you succeed, you may wed my daughter. If not, you must prepare a feast for my family and then never come back here again."

The young man agreed. For two days, he stood in the freezing water. Near the end of the test, he saw a house catch fire in the distance. He pointed his arm toward the fire.

"Aha!" the rich man cried. "You have failed the test!"

The young man started to argue. That fire was too far away to give him any warmth. But then he had an idea.

The next day, the young man prepared a wonderful feast for the family. But he did not add salt to any of the food.

When the father tasted the first dish, he spat the food out. "Where's the salt?" he demanded.

The young man pointed to a dish of salt. It was on another table. He explained, "You said the fire gave me warmth from a hill far away. In the same way, that dish of salt gives flavor to the soup."

The father realized that the young man was wise and clever. He said, "Very well! You have proved yourself worthy of my daughter."

So the young man married the daughter, and the match was a good one.

1. How was the father in this story like the young man?

Ⓐ He was a farmer.

Ⓑ He was poor once.

Ⓒ He passed a test.

Ⓓ He had lots of money.

2. To pass the test, the young man had to—

Ⓐ prepare a feast for the girl's family.

Ⓑ save a house from burning.

Ⓒ prove that he knew how to use salt.

Ⓓ stand in freezing water without moving.

3. The rich man is best described as—

Ⓐ protective of his daughter but fair.

Ⓑ greedy and mean to the young man.

Ⓒ angry and hard to get along with.

Ⓓ trusting and kind to everyone.

4. What is the theme of this story?

Ⓐ Don't wait until tomorrow to do the things you can do today.

Ⓑ If at first you don't succeed, then try again.

Ⓒ If you don't want anyone to know what you did, then don't do it.

Ⓓ Teach a man to fish, and he'll be able to feed himself.

GO ON

Read this passage. Then answer questions 5–8 by filling in the circle next to the best answer.

Bread

Bread comes in many shapes and sizes. In parts of Asia, people cook thin, round breads over a fire. In Africa, some bread is sour and spongy. Some bakers in Italy make bread without salt. The French make flaky rolls. Yellow cornbread is popular in some places. People like round and chewy bagels, too.

In the United States, most kinds of bread are made with yeast. When yeast combines with warm water and sugar, tiny air bubbles form. The baker then uses the yeast mixture and flour to make dough. The bubbles get trapped in the dough. Then the dough rises, or expands. Finally, the dough goes in an oven to bake. The smell of bread fills the air.

The breads we buy most often are made with wheat, rye, or oat flour. But for some breads, we use special ingredients. In the summer, for example, some people like to make zucchini bread. Zucchini is a kind of squash. In the fall, people make pumpkin bread. These kinds of bread are made with flour. But they do not contain yeast. So they are heavier than most breads.

The smell of bread can make almost anyone hungry. Bread is often called "the food of life." The first bread was baked about 6,000 years ago in Egypt. Since then, bread has been enjoyed all over the world.

5. What is the main idea of this passage?

Ⓐ Bread comes in many shapes and sizes.

Ⓑ Most kinds of bread are made with yeast.

Ⓒ For some breads, we use special ingredients.

Ⓓ The first bread was baked 6,000 years ago in Egypt.

6. How is zucchini bread different from most kinds of bread?

Ⓐ Zucchini bread is baked in an oven.

Ⓑ It has a pleasant smell.

Ⓒ Zucchini bread is not made with yeast.

Ⓓ It contains a lot of sugar.

7. Yeast causes bread dough to—

Ⓐ taste better.

Ⓑ smell good.

Ⓒ rise and expand.

Ⓓ turn brown.

8. Which sentence best summarizes this passage?

Ⓐ In Asia, people make thin, round bread.

Ⓑ Most breads are made with flour.

Ⓒ In the fall, people make pumpkin bread.

Ⓓ People all over the world make and eat bread.

GO ON

Read this passage. Then answer questions 9–14 by filling in the circle next to the best answer.

Being Roberto Clemente

My name is Roberto. I was named after the baseball star, Roberto Clemente. It's too bad I can't catch or throw.

Last month at school, we put on a play about Clemente's life. My teacher asked me to play the part of Clemente, and I accepted. At least I didn't have to catch a ball!

A week after the play, I was walking down the street. I passed a parking lot where some kids were playing baseball. One boy slid into first base and skinned his leg on the pavement. He had to leave the game.

Ramon, one of my classmates, called to me. "Hey, Roberto Clemente! We need another player. Come on over!"

Ramon didn't know how bad an athlete I was, but I liked Ramon. When I walked over, the kids cheered. The game was tied, and Ramon's team really wanted to win.

I took the injured boy's place at first base. When Ramon hit the ball, I ran all the way to home plate. The kids on my team yelled and screamed.

When it was our turn in the field, Ramon tossed me a glove. He said, "Come on, you'll be great!"

It was the last inning. The other team had two runners on base and two outs. I was playing center field. When the ball flew toward me, I held up the glove. I half expected the ball to hit me in the head. But instead I felt a hard slap on my hand. When I looked inside the glove, the ball was there!

All of my teammates surrounded me. I heard someone say, "Way to go, Roberto!"

I'm not Roberto Clemente. But for once I knew what it was like to be a star.

9. Which event happened *first*?

Ⓒ Roberto ran to home plate.

Ⓓ A boy hurt his leg.

Ⓔ Roberto's class put on a play.

Ⓕ Ramon asked Roberto to play baseball.

10. What is the main problem in this story?

Ⓒ Roberto cannot get a good part in a play.

Ⓓ He misses the ball when he plays in a baseball game.

Ⓔ Roberto does not like his name.

Ⓕ The kids playing baseball need another player.

11. Where does this story take place?

Ⓒ in a parking lot

Ⓓ on a school bus

Ⓔ on a school playground

Ⓕ in a baseball stadium

GO ON

12. How does the game end?

Ⓐ Ramon hits the ball.

Ⓑ The other team scores.

Ⓒ A boy skins his leg.

Ⓓ Roberto catches the ball.

13. How does Roberto feel when the game ends?

Ⓐ embarrassed

Ⓑ worried

Ⓒ surprised

Ⓓ disappointed

14. Which sentence best describes Roberto?

Ⓐ He is not a very good team member, but he loves to play.

Ⓑ He is willing to do something difficult even though he might fail.

Ⓒ He is willing to study hard, but he does not enjoy sports.

Ⓓ He is not very well liked because he is conceited and selfish.

Read this passage. Then answer questions 15–20 by filling in the circle next to the best answer.

Bear Man

One day in New Hampshire, Ben Kilham found two bear cubs alone in the woods. They were about nine weeks old. The mother bear was gone. The two cubs were hugging each other to keep warm. Ben is a scientist who studies bears. He knew the cubs would not survive. So he took them home.

The cubs weighed less than four pounds each. He fed them sheep's milk and applesauce, and the cubs followed him around like puppies.

When the cubs grew bigger, Ben took them into the woods. He wanted to help them learn how to find food and fend for themselves. So he began teaching them as a mother bear would do.

Like a mother bear, Ben took the cubs on long walks in the woods. He played with them along the way. They tore apart rotten logs to find ants and grubs. They climbed trees and tasted flowers. Ben showed them where to find berries and tasty plants.

At the same time, Ben learned a lot about bears from observing the cubs. He saw them bite or rub their backs on some of the trees. They were leaving their scent on the bark. Other bears would know who had been there.

GO ON

When winter came, Ben made a den for the two cubs. They would sleep there until the snows melted. When spring arrived, Ben waited outside the den. Like a mother bear, he needed to guide them as they came out of hibernation.

Bear cubs usually leave their mothers after a year and a half. That's what these cubs did. When Ben returned home, the cubs went off to live in the forest.

So far, Ben the "Bear Man" has raised 35 bear cubs.

15. How does Ben Kilham act like a mother bear?

Ⓐ He teaches the cubs how to find food.

Ⓑ He weighs as much as a mother bear.

Ⓒ He rubs trees to send messages to other bears.

Ⓓ He feeds them the same foods that cubs eat.

16. Why were the bear cubs hugging each other when Ben found them in the forest?

Ⓐ They were frightened.

Ⓑ They were hungry.

Ⓒ They were cold.

Ⓓ They were playing.

17. What problem did the bear cubs have when Ben found them?

Ⓐ Both of the cubs were injured.

Ⓑ They were afraid of humans.

Ⓒ They didn't know how to climb trees.

Ⓓ The mother bear had left them.

18. How did Ben help the cubs learn to survive?

    Ⓐ He fed them applesauce and sheep's milk.

    Ⓑ He showed them how to leave messages on a tree.

    Ⓒ He made a den for them.

    Ⓓ He showed them plants and berries they could eat.

19. What did Ben learn from the cubs?

    Ⓐ Bears leave messages on the trees.

    Ⓑ Mother bears do not take care of their babies.

    Ⓒ Rotten logs often have ants in them.

    Ⓓ Bears sleep through the winter.

20. Which sentence best summarizes this passage?

    Ⓐ Bear cubs need their mothers until they are 18 months old.

    Ⓑ Ben Kilham raises bear cubs and teaches them to survive.

    Ⓒ Bears leave messages on trees by biting and rubbing the bark.

    Ⓓ A mother bear leaves her cubs alone to see if they can survive.

GO ON

Vocabulary/Word Study

Read each question and choose the best answer. Fill in the circle next to the answer you choose.

21. The young man married the daughter, and the match was a good one.

What is the meaning of *match* in this sentence?

Ⓐ a thing that looks like something else

Ⓑ a contest or game

Ⓒ a union or marriage

Ⓓ a wooden stick used to start a fire

22. When yeast combines with warm water and sugar, tiny air bubbles form.

Which word is a synonym for *combines*?

Ⓐ bakes   Ⓒ explodes

Ⓑ separates   Ⓓ mixes

23. My teacher asked me to play the part of Clemente, and I accepted.

Which word is an antonym for *accepted*?

Ⓐ learned   Ⓒ improved

Ⓑ refused   Ⓓ changed

24. Roberto played well in the last inning.

What is the correct plural form of <u>inning</u>?

Ⓐ innings   Ⓒ inningses

Ⓑ inning's   Ⓓ inninges

25. Ben learned a lot about bears by observing the cubs.

What does *observing* mean?

(A) watching   (C) training

(B) feeding   (D) finding

26. A dictionary page has the guide words *eight/elbow*.

Which word would be on the same page?

(A) ember   (C) eject

(B) even   (D) ending

27. Which of these words can be changed to an adjective by adding the suffix *-able*?

(A) paper   (C) soon

(B) them   (D) adjust

28. White snow covers the field.

Which word is in the same word family as *covers*?

(A) colors   (C) discover

(B) over   (D) love

29. Which verb form best fits in this sentence?

For now, we are _____ the good weather.

(A) enjoy   (C) enjoys

(B) enjoying   (D) enjoyed

30. My little sister rides her tricycle on the sidewalk.

The word *tricycle* contains the Greek root *cycle*, meaning—

(A) leg.   (C) fast.

(B) three.   (D) wheel.

GO ON

Grammar, Usage, and Mechanics

The following is a rough draft of a student's story. It contains errors. Read the draft. Then read each question and decide which is the best answer. Fill in the circle next to the answer you choose.

Pizza Night

(1) At our house, Friday night is pizza night. (2) No one wants to cook, so we order pizza. (3) After dinner we play board games.

(4) For a long time, us ordered only cheese pizza. (5) Then one week Dad surprised us with pepperoni. (6) After that we changed each week: one week cheese, the next week pepperoni.

(7) Then one night, Mom was looking at a menu from the pizza place. (8) "Maybe we should try a Hawaiian pizza. (9) It's made with pineapple and ham."

(10) "Yuck," I said, "I couldn't never eat that. (11) Next week we're supposed to get pepperoni!"

(12) "Aren't you getting tired of the same old thing? Dad asked." (13) He wanted to try pizza with chicken and broccoli. (14) But that sounded like a regular old weeknight dinner to me.

(15) We played a board game that night. (16) It was so much fun that I almost forgot about the weird pizzas. (17) Almost, but not completely.

(18) On the next Friday night, we had a family vote and ended up with a Hawaiian pizza. (19) Well, I was hungry and the pizza didn't smell too bad, so I tried it. (20) It was not the <u>most great</u> pizza I've ever had, but it was pretty good.

31. What is the correct way to write sentence 4?

(A) For a long time, her ordered only cheese pizza.

(B) For a long time, me ordered only cheese pizza.

(C) For a long time, we ordered only cheese pizza.

(D) Leave as is.

32. What is the correct way to write sentence 10?

(A) "Yuck," I said, "I could not never eat that.

(B) "Yuck," I said, "I could never eat that.

(C) "Yuck," I said, "I couldn't not ever eat that.

(D) Leave as is.

33. What is the correct way to punctuate sentence 12?

(A) "Aren't you getting tired of the same old thing?" Dad asked.

(B) "Aren't you getting tired of the same old thing"? Dad asked.

(C) Aren't you getting tired of the same old thing? "Dad asked."

(D) Leave as is.

34. Which of these is a sentence fragment?

(A) Next week we're supposed to get pepperoni!

(B) We played a board game that night.

(C) It was so much fun that I almost forgot about the weird pizzas.

(D) Almost, but not completely.

35. What is the correct way to write the underlined part of sentence 20?

(A) more great

(B) greater

(C) greatest

(D) Leave as is.

GO ON

231

The following is a rough draft of a student's report. It contains errors. Read the draft. Then read each question and decide which is the best answer. Fill in the circle next to the answer you choose.

The Hoover Dam

(1) In the early 1900s, thousands of people moved to the western United States. (2) But a large part of the West was a desert. (3) There was not enough water for all the people.

(4) The U.S. government decided to solve this problem by building a dam on the Colorado River. (5) The Colorado flows 1,450 miles from the Rocky Mountains to the sea. (6) Engineers explored the river to find the best place for a dam. (7) Finally, they chose Boulder Canyon. (8) Not far from the city of Las Vegas.

(9) Workers began building the Hoover Dam in 1930 and completed it in 1935. (10) This was one of the greatest public works projects in history. (11) About 16,000 people worked on the dam. (12) More than 100 workers lives were lost. (13) But the benefits of the project were great.

(14) The dam controlled the flow of the Colorado River, and it created a huge lake called Lake Mead. (15) That lake is 115 miles long and very deep. (16) Water from the river is used to irrigate farmland. (17) Water from the river flows to cities, too. (18) The river provides water for more than 25 million people.

36. Which numbered sentence is a compound sentence?

    Ⓐ sentence 3   Ⓒ sentence 6

    Ⓑ sentence 4   Ⓓ sentence 14

37. What is the correct way to write the underlined word in sentence 7?

  Ⓐ Most final,   Ⓒ More finally,

  Ⓑ Final,   Ⓓ Leave as is.

38. How can sentence 8 be written correctly?

  Ⓐ Being not far from the city of Las Vegas.

  Ⓑ It is not far from the city of Las Vegas.

  Ⓒ There, not far from the city of Las Vegas.

  Ⓓ Leave as is.

39. What is the correct way to write the underlined word in sentence 12?

  Ⓐ worker's   Ⓒ workers's

  Ⓑ workers'   Ⓓ Leave as is.

40. How can sentences 17 and 18 best be combined?

  Ⓐ Water from the river flows to cities, too, providing water for more than 25 million people.

  Ⓑ Water from the river flows to cities; however, the river provides water for more than 25 million people.

  Ⓒ Water from the river flows to cities, too, since the river provides water for more than 25 million people.

  Ⓓ For more than 25 million people, water from the river flows to cities, too, and provides water.

Writing

Read the prompt. Write your essay on the lines below and on the next page, or on the answer document.

Write a personal narrative telling about a time when you did something exciting with a friend.

When you write your personal narrative, remember to
- tell what happened in order,
- include descriptive language and sensory details to make your narrative interesting, and
- use correct grammar, spelling, punctuation, and capitalization.

_____

_____

_____

_____

_____

_____

_____

_____

_____

_____

GO ON

Listening

Listen to each passage as your teacher reads it aloud. Then listen to the questions. Choose the best answer to each question. Fill in the circle beside the answer you choose.

41. Ⓐ on a soccer field

Ⓑ in a school gym

Ⓒ on a playground

Ⓓ in a classroom

42. Ⓐ Pete tries to do the rope climb.

Ⓑ Pete starts going to a new school.

Ⓒ Pete gets to know Joe Logan.

Ⓓ Pete and his mom move from Texas.

43. Ⓐ He does not want to climb the rope.

Ⓑ He does not have any friends.

Ⓒ He does not get along with Mr. Riley.

Ⓓ He does not like his new school.

44. Ⓐ Pete fails the rope climb.

Ⓑ Mr. Riley shakes Pete's hand.

Ⓒ Joe Logan congratulates Pete.

Ⓓ Pete hurts his back in the gym.

45. Ⓐ relieved

Ⓑ worried

Ⓒ embarrassed

Ⓓ disappointed

46.
(A) Spanish explorers

(B) where tomatoes came from

(C) deadly nightshade

(D) how tomatoes are grown

47.
(A) Spain

(B) England

(C) Peru and Mexico

(D) Italy

48.
(A) They are all poisonous.

(B) They all came from Mexico.

(C) They are used to make spaghetti.

(D) They are not native to the United States.

49.
(A) Tomatoes are related to deadly nightshade.

(B) They came from South America.

(C) Tomato plants were pretty to look at.

(D) They were grown in England.

50.
(A) Tomatoes are used to make salads, pizza, and spaghetti sauce.

(B) We eat millions of tons of tomatoes every year.

(C) Tomatoes came to the United States from Europe in the 1700s.

(D) Spanish explorers found many plants they had never seen before.

STOP

NAME _____ DATE _____

READ180

rSkills® Midyear Test (Level b)

DIRECTIONS: This is a test of reading, writing, and listening. Follow the directions for each part of the test, and choose the best answer to each question.

SAMPLE QUESTIONS

Amazing Trees

Three of the most remarkable trees in the world all grow in California. For example, the tallest tree in the world is a California redwood. It stands more than 370 feet high. The largest tree is a sequoia named General Sherman. It weighs 2.7 million pounds. The oldest tree is a pine named Methuselah. It has been growing more than 4,800 years.

Sample A. What is this passage mostly about?

Ⓐ people in California

Ⓑ a man named General Sherman

Ⓒ saving the rainforest

Ⓓ three remarkable trees

Sample B. The tallest tree in the world is a California redwood.

Which word is a synonym for the word *tallest*?

Ⓐ amazing   Ⓒ heavy

Ⓑ highest   Ⓓ oldest

See p. 299
for scoring.

Go on to the next page to begin the test.

239

Comprehension

Read this passage. Then answer questions 1–6 by filling in the circle next to the best answer.

The Bear and the Farmer

One day, a farmer planted some turnip seeds in a field in the forest. He worked hard, digging and planting. He weeded the garden and brought water from a nearby stream. All that summer the farmer worked, and a bear watched the plants grow.

In the fall, the bear saw the farmer harvest the crop. He said, "Give me some of those turnips, or I forbid you ever to enter my forest again."

The farmer smiled and said, "That's only fair. This is your land, so we should divide my crop between us. You can take the green tops, and I will keep the roots."

The bear agreed. So the farmer gave the bear all the turnip tops, which seemed to be the best bargain. The farmer loaded the roots in his cart and drove away.

A bird flew down and told the bear, "You silly beast! The roots are the sweetest and most nutritious part of the turnip. That farmer tricked you!"

The next spring, the farmer returned to the field to plant some wheat. He plowed the soil and sowed the seeds in the spring. In the fall, the bear was waiting for the farmer to harvest the wheat.

"You tricked me once, but you will not trick me this time!" said the bear.

The farmer replied, "I understand your point. This time I will let you choose what part of the plant you want, the root or the plant. I want to be fair and give you your share."

So the bear chose the roots of the wheat plants. The farmer gave the roots to the bear after he harvested the golden stalks of wheat. Then he loaded the stalks in his cart and drove away. The bear sat on the ground and began chewing the roots of the wheat, but they were tasteless and dry.

The same bird flew by and said, "The farmer tricked you again! The roots of the wheat plant are useless. Most farmers leave them in the field to rot."

The bear became angry at his own foolishness and at the dishonest farmer who had tricked him again. From that time on, wild bears and humans have not gotten along very well.

1. What happens *first* in this story?

Ⓐ The farmer weeds his garden.

Ⓑ A bear watches the plants grow.

Ⓒ The farmer plants some turnip seeds.

Ⓓ A bear asks for some food.

2. Where does this story take place?

Ⓐ in a forest

Ⓑ on an island

Ⓒ in a desert

Ⓓ near a lake

3. What is the main problem in this story?

Ⓐ The bear wants a share of the farmer's crop.

Ⓑ The farmer does not have enough crops to take to market.

Ⓒ The wild animals try to eat the farmer's crops.

Ⓓ The bear is lazy and does not want to help the farmer.

4. Which words best describe the farmer?

Ⓐ hard-working and honest

Ⓑ angry and mean

Ⓒ generous and kind

Ⓓ sneaky and clever

GO ON

5. How does the farmer trick the bear?

Ⓐ He lets the bear take last year's crop.

Ⓑ He gives the bear the useless part of each crop.

Ⓒ He asks the bird to give the bear a message.

Ⓓ He tells the bear to come back after the harvest.

6. Why is the bear upset with himself at the end?

Ⓐ He has no food for the winter.

Ⓑ The bird makes fun of him.

Ⓒ The farmer has tricked him twice.

Ⓓ He does not even like turnips.

Read this passage. Then answer questions 7–12 by filling in the circle next to the best answer.

Farmers in Despair

Life was hard for everyone in the United States during the Great Depression. Factories, stores, and banks shut down. Workers lost their jobs and their homes. But people in the southern Great Plains suffered more than most. In this area, money troubles combined with nature to create a disaster.

Out of Money, Out of Luck

When the Great Depression began in 1929, farming was the main way of life in the southern Great Plains. But the farmers could not sell the food they produced. They tried reducing their prices, but no one had any money. Each day, the farmers' problems grew. They could not afford to buy seeds for new crops. They could not buy tools and equipment. They could not pay their helpers.

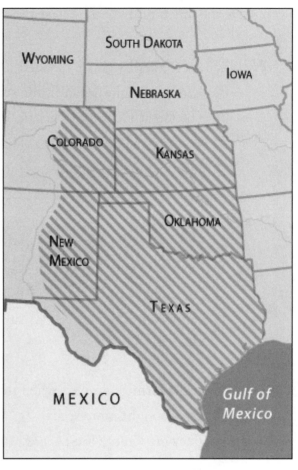

The Southern Great Plains

Years of Drought and Wind

Two years later, forces of nature also turned against the farmers. In 1931, a drought began. For seven years, little rain fell in the southern Great Plains. Unwise farming practices had already made farm soil loose and dry. The lack of rain made this problem much worse. Then, between 1934 and 1938, fierce windstorms struck the region. Each storm swept up the loose, dry soil and carried it away. People and animals caught outdoors in a storm were blinded or choked by the dust. Blowing dust piled up in homes and barns and had to be shoveled out. It wrecked the engines of cars and farm vehicles.

In only a few years, the storms took away the topsoil from 50 million acres of farmland. The area became known as the Dust Bowl. Farmers could no longer make a living there. Thousands of farm families had to move away and start over again.

GO ON

Never Again

Farmers of the southern Great Plains learned a hard lesson from the Dust Bowl. They now know better ways to plow and plant their fields. They plant trees to keep the soil from blowing away, and they take better care of the land. Today's farmers hope never to relive the tough times of the Great Depression.

7. Which of these events happened *first*?

Ⓐ A long drought began in the southern Great Plains.

Ⓑ The Great Depression began.

Ⓒ Windstorms blew through the southern Great Plains.

Ⓓ Farm families moved away from the Dust Bowl.

8. What is the main idea of this passage?

Ⓐ Everyone had a hard time during the Great Depression.

Ⓑ Farming was an important way of life in some parts of the United States.

Ⓒ For seven years, little rain fell in the southern Great Plains.

Ⓓ Farmers of the southern Great Plains suffered a lot during the Great Depression.

9. What did farmers do next when they could not sell their crops?

Ⓐ They bought more seeds.

Ⓑ They grew more food.

Ⓒ They lowered their prices.

Ⓓ They paid their helpers.

10. What lesson did farmers in the southern Great Plains learn from the events of the 1930s?

Ⓐ They should take better care of farmland.

Ⓑ Cars and trucks can be ruined by dust.

Ⓒ They should buy better seeds and tools.

Ⓓ Windstorms and droughts can happen anytime.

11. Today's farmers plant trees on their farms mainly to—

Ⓐ make farmland more attractive.

Ⓑ give crops enough shade to grow.

Ⓒ keep soil from blowing away.

Ⓓ mark the borders between farms.

12. Which sentence best summarizes this passage?

Ⓐ During the Great Depression, farmers faced money problems and droughts.

Ⓑ The land in the southern Great Plains became known as the Dust Bowl.

Ⓒ Today's farmers don't want to relive the bad times of the Great Depression.

Ⓓ During the Great Depression, many factories, stores, and banks shut down.

GO ON

Read this poem. Then answer questions 13–16 by filling in the circle next to the best answer.

Moment of Truth

The long hallway stretches ahead.
It gleams with a fresh coat of wax
as bright and hopeful as the promise
I made myself last night.

This year I will fit in.
People will know my name.
I won't sit with the losers at lunch.
I will belong somewhere.

Now comes the moment of truth.
Leon ambles through the crowd.
Everyone calls out to him:
"Hey, Leon, what's up, man?"

I hear myself say the same words,
but my voice breaks and cracks,
as high and thin as my sister's.
I want to hide inside my locker.

Leon's friends glare at me.
They get ready to toss an insult,
something that will sting like a slap
and show me not to talk to Leon.

But Leon speaks first.
"Hey, Duane, what's up yourself?"
He nods and almost smiles,
then heads off down the hallway.

13. The action of this poem takes place in a—

    Ⓐ store.

    Ⓑ mall.

    Ⓒ restaurant.

    Ⓓ school.

14. What does Duane do *first*?

    Ⓐ He says hello to Leon.

    Ⓑ He makes a promise to himself.

    Ⓒ He hides in his locker.

    Ⓓ He walks out of the school.

15. Which sentence best describes Duane?

    Ⓐ He is afraid of Leon.

    Ⓑ He thinks he is special.

    Ⓒ He feels sorry for Leon.

    Ⓓ He is unsure of himself.

16. What happens at the end of this poem?

    Ⓐ Leon speaks to Duane.

    Ⓑ Leon ignores Duane.

    Ⓒ Leon's friends insult Duane.

    Ⓓ Duane and Leon become best friends.

GO ON

Read this passage. Then answer questions 17–20 by filling in the circle next to the best answer.

Water Bottles

If you want a drink of water, there are several ways to get it. You can pour a glass from a tap. You can drink from a fountain. Or you can reach for that bottle of water you probably have with you.

More Bottles Every Year

Not so long ago, bottled water wasn't widely available. Today, however, plastic water bottles seem to be everywhere. Bottled water began to catch on in the United States around 1980. That year, about 600,000 gallons were sold. Over the next 25 years, sales of water bottles skyrocketed. In 2005, Americans bought more than 7.5 billion gallons of bottled water. So far, sales are not slowing down.

Environmental Issues

It's easy to see why bottled water sells. Water is good for you. The bottles are handy and easy to carry. However, bottled water also creates problems for the environment. The more bottled water we drink, the bigger the problems get.

The problems boil down to one word: WASTE. Although plastic water bottles can be recycled, most are not. Instead they end up in landfills where they take 400 years to break down! Plastic bottles are also a waste of oil. Crude oil is used to make plastic. If the oil used for plastic bottles were made into fuel instead, it would keep 100,000 American cars running for a year. Finally, think about all the fuel used to truck water bottles to the stores. Clearly, water bottles cause all kinds of waste.

Saving Plastic

Some people are trying to stop the waste. In 2006, the mayor of Salt Lake City took steps to limit city workers' use of bottled water. He asked them to drink tap water instead. In 2007, San Francisco's mayor banned the purchase of bottled water for city offices. Officials in New York City and Minneapolis have also asked people to drink more tap water and less bottled water. Slowly, the tide is turning against plastic water bottles.

17. What is the main idea of this passage?

Ⓐ Many people carry water with them in plastic bottles.

Ⓑ Sales of bottled water keep growing every year.

Ⓒ Bottled water is popular, but the bottles create waste.

Ⓓ You can drink water from a tap, a fountain, or a bottle.

18. Why are plastic bottles bad for the environment?

Ⓐ They hold only small amounts of water.

Ⓑ They are handy and easy to carry.

Ⓒ They keep American cars running.

Ⓓ They cause all kinds of waste.

19. According to this passage, what is one problem with bottled water?

Ⓐ There isn't enough for everyone.

Ⓑ It has a bad taste.

Ⓒ Most bottles do not get recycled.

Ⓓ It costs too much.

20. Which sentence best summarizes the last part of this passage?

Ⓐ Some leaders are trying to limit bottles and the waste they cause.

Ⓑ Plastic water bottles take 400 years to break down.

Ⓒ Most people drink water from plastic bottles when they're thirsty.

Ⓓ Oil is used to make plastic bottles and to fuel American cars.

GO ON

Vocabulary/Word Study

Read each question and choose the best answer. Fill in the circle next to the answer you choose.

21. Leon ambles through the crowd.

    What does the word *ambles* mean in this sentence?

    Ⓐ shouts   Ⓒ rides

    Ⓑ walks   Ⓓ looks

22. My friend Duane likes to daydream during classes.

    Which word in the sentence is a compound word?

    Ⓐ friend   Ⓒ during

    Ⓑ daydream   Ⓓ classes

23. The bear waited for the farmer to harvest the wheat.

    Which word is a synonym for *harvest*?

    Ⓐ plant   Ⓒ sell

    Ⓑ cook   Ⓓ pick

24. The farmers *reduced* their prices.

    Which word is an antonym for *reduced*?

    Ⓐ lowered   Ⓒ raised

    Ⓑ charged   Ⓓ defended

25. They do not see eye to eye on the subject of bottled water.

    What does the idiom "see eye to eye" mean in this sentence?

    Ⓐ agree with each other   Ⓒ look at each other

    Ⓑ speak clearly   Ⓓ make sense

26. That new building is a huge structure made of steel and glass.

Which of these words is *not* in the same word family as *structure*?

Ⓐ structural
Ⓒ trucker

Ⓑ destruction
Ⓓ construct

27. Mr. James is the narrator of the story.

What does *narrator* mean in this sentence?

Ⓐ narrate well

Ⓑ person who narrates

Ⓒ narrate again

Ⓓ able to narrate

28. Shawna wants to revisit the space museum.

In this sentence, *revisit* means—

Ⓐ visit again.
Ⓒ visit before.

Ⓑ not visit.
Ⓓ able to visit.

29. In which sentence is *weak* used correctly?

Ⓐ We went away last <u>weak</u>.

Ⓑ Aunt Mina stayed with us for a <u>weak</u>.

Ⓒ Maria says she feels <u>weak</u> today.

Ⓓ Saturday is the best day of the <u>weak</u>.

30. In which sentence is *heel* used correctly?

Ⓐ That cut will <u>heel</u> quickly.

Ⓑ <u>Heel</u> call us at five o'clock.

Ⓒ His arm did not <u>heel</u> well.

Ⓓ The <u>heel</u> of my foot hurts.

GO ON

Grammar, Usage, and Mechanics

The following is a rough draft of a student's journal entry. It contains errors. Read the draft. Then read each question and decide which is the best answer. Fill in the circle next to the answer you choose.

May 11, 1934

(1) I sitting am at the kitchen table writing in this diary. (2) I had to light a candle even though it's the middle of the day. (3) There is something strange going on outside.

(4) Things have been bad on our farm in Oklahoma for a couple of years. (5) Dad says it's this Depression. (6) Used to pay high prices for our grain. (7) Now they are all out of work.

(8) At first we had plenty of food to feed ourselves. (9) But then the rains just stopped, and the land got drier and drier. (10) Some days, when the wind <u>blowed</u> hard, it lifted dust off the dry fields and flung it into the air.

(11) Ma hated that, especially when she had clean clothes hanging outside on the clothesline. (12) Dad hated it even more. (13) "If this keeps up, the wind will blow away all of our good, rich topsoil," he said. (14) "How can we grow anything then."

(15) The dust kept getting worse. (16) Nothing had prepared us for this storm. (17) The wind started blowing really hard. (18) Then we saw a black cloud approaching. (19) When the cloud reached us, it blotted out all the light of the sun. (20) It was morning, but everything went dark.

31. Which is the correct way to write sentence 1?

(A) I sitting am at the table kitchen writing in this diary.

(B) I am sitting at the table kitchen writing in this diary.

(C) I am sitting at the kitchen table writing in this diary.

(D) Leave as is.

32. Sentence 6 is a sentence fragment. Which is the best way to correct it?

(A) People used to pay high prices for our grain.

(B) Were used to paying high prices for our grain.

(C) Used to paying high prices for our grain.

(D) For our grain, used to pay high prices.

33. Which is the correct way to write the underlined word in sentence 10?

(A) blow

(B) blew

(C) blowing

(D) blewed

34. Which is the correct way to punctuate sentence 14?

(A) "How can we grow anything then!"

(B) "How can we grow anything then"

(C) "How can we grow anything then?"

(D) Leave as is.

35. How can sentences 15 and 16 best be combined?

(A) The dust kept getting worse, so nothing had prepared us for this storm.

(B) The dust kept getting worse, with nothing preparing us for this storm.

(C) The dust kept getting worse, since nothing had prepared us for this storm.

(D) The dust kept getting worse, but nothing had prepared us for this storm.

GO ON

The following is a rough draft of a student's report. It contains errors. Read the draft. Then read each question and decide which is the best answer. Fill in the circle next to the answer you choose.

Wildfires of 2007

(1) When we think of wildfires, we often think of the American West. (2) We picture forests blazing in California Arizona and Idaho. (3) However, some of the worst forest fires in 2007 did not take place in the United States. (4) They occurred in Greece.

(5) The first major fire <u>started</u> on June 28, 2007, in a Greek national park. (6) In just a few days, almost 14,000 acres were destroyed. (7) By the middle of July, the problem had spread. (8) More than 100 fires had broken out, including some just outside Athens, the capital of the country. (9) Villages, forests, and farms were destroyed.

(10) The worst disaster occurred in August. (11) Dozens of new fires broke out. (12) They caused Prime Minister Kostas Karamanlis to declare a state of emergency. (13) Many parts of the country were in danger, <u>including mount Olympus</u>, the birthplace of the first Olympic Games.

(14) Fortunately, nations all over the world provided assistance. (15) Canada sent special airplanes that drop water on fires. (16) France offered 60 firefighters and six fire trucks, and Norway supplied a firefighting helicopter. (17) Many historic places were saved.

(18) By the end of August, temperatures and winds had dropped firefighters gained control of the situation. (19) The fires had caused billions of dollars of damage.

36. Which is the correct way to punctuate sentence 2?

Ⓐ We picture forests blazing in California, Arizona, and, Idaho.

Ⓑ We picture forests blazing in California, Arizona, and Idaho.

Ⓒ We picture forests blazing, in California, Arizona and Idaho.

Ⓓ We picture forests blazing in California Arizona, and Idaho.

37. Which is the correct way to write the underlined verb in sentence 5?

Ⓐ start   Ⓒ will start

Ⓑ starting   Ⓓ Leave as is.

38. Which is the best way to combine sentences 11 and 12?

Ⓐ Dozens of new fires broke out, causing Prime Minister Kostas Karamanlis to declare a state of emergency.

Ⓑ Dozens of new fires broke out, with Prime Minister Kostas Karamanlis declaring a state of emergency.

Ⓒ Dozens of new fires broke out, caused Prime Minister Kostas Karamanlis to declare a state of emergency.

Ⓓ Dozens of new fires breaking out and causing Prime Minister Kostas Karamanlis to declare a state of emergency.

39. What is the correct way to write the underlined part of sentence 13?

Ⓐ including mount olympus

Ⓑ including Mount olympus

Ⓒ including Mount Olympus

Ⓓ Leave as is.

40. How should sentence 18 be written correctly?

Ⓐ By the end of August, temperatures and winds had dropped, and firefighters gained control of the situation.

Ⓑ By the end of August, temperatures and winds had dropped, firefighters gained control of the situation.

Ⓒ By the end of August, temperatures, and winds had dropped firefighters, gained control of the situation.

Ⓓ By the end of August, temperatures and winds had dropped, but firefighters gained control of the situation.

GO ON

Writing

Read the prompt. Write your essay on the lines below and on the next page, or on the answer document.

Explain why going to live in another country might be difficult—and exciting.

When you write your essay, remember to
- state the main topic,
- include details that support the main idea, and
- use correct grammar, spelling, punctuation, and capitalization.

_____

_____

_____

_____

_____

_____

_____

_____

_____

_____

_____

_____

_____

GO ON

Listening

Listen to each passage as your teacher reads it aloud. Then listen to the questions. Choose the best answer to each question. Fill in the circle beside the answer you choose.

41.
  Ⓐ She takes a math test.
  Ⓑ She goes to the library.
  Ⓒ She sleeps a little late.
  Ⓓ She looks through a dictionary.

42.
  Ⓐ Her mother is upset with her.
  Ⓑ She cannot find her homework.
  Ⓒ Her mother makes her eat breakfast.
  Ⓓ She does not have a dictionary.

43.
  Ⓐ at school
  Ⓑ at the library
  Ⓒ at home
  Ⓓ at the bank

44.
  Ⓐ worried
  Ⓑ cautious
  Ⓒ guilty
  Ⓓ surprised

45.
  Ⓐ The librarian keeps all the money.
  Ⓑ Isabel gets a reward.
  Ⓒ Mrs. Charles calls Isabel at home.
  Ⓓ Isabel spends all the money.

46. Ⓐ living in Costa Rica

Ⓑ the life of Franklin Chang-Diaz

Ⓒ schools in Hartford, Connecticut

Ⓓ Franklin Chang-Diaz's family

47. Ⓐ Franklin moved to the United States.

Ⓑ Franklin won a scholarship to study science.

Ⓒ Franklin applied to become an astronaut.

Ⓓ Franklin took a job as a scientist.

48. Ⓐ He was often homesick.

Ⓑ He did not have a place to live.

Ⓒ He could not speak English.

Ⓓ He wanted to give up his dream.

49. Ⓐ He was the first Latino astronaut.

Ⓑ He was born in 1950 in Costa Rica.

Ⓒ He was named after a president.

Ⓓ He thought about outer space as a boy.

50. Ⓐ Franklin Chang-Diaz moved to Hartford, Connecticut.

Ⓑ Franklin Chang-Diaz was born in Costa Rica but now lives in the United States.

Ⓒ Franklin Chang-Diaz was born in 1950 and retired in 2005.

Ⓓ Franklin Chang-Diaz worked hard to become an astronaut.

NAME _____   DATE _____

rSkills® End-of-Year Test (Level b)

DIRECTIONS: This is a test of reading, writing, and listening. Follow the directions for each part of the test, and choose the best answer to each question.

SAMPLE QUESTIONS

The Golden Spike

In the 1800s, many Americans wanted to move to California. Traveling by wagon took a long time, and the trip was dangerous. People dreamed of a railroad that would cross the United States. In 1865, two companies began to build such a railroad. One group started laying track in the East, and one started in the West. Four years later, the two groups met in Utah. The two tracks were joined with a special golden spike, and the railroad was complete.

Sample A. What is this passage mostly about?

Ⓐ building a railroad across the United States

Ⓑ traveling to California by wagon

Ⓒ differences between the East and the West

Ⓓ a dangerous trip to California

Sample B. The two tracks were joined with a special golden spike.

Which word is an antonym for the word *joined*?

Ⓐ built   Ⓒ separated

Ⓑ painted   Ⓓ prepared

See p. 300
for scoring.

Go on to the next page to begin the test.

Comprehension

Read this passage. Then answer questions 1–4 by filling in the circle next to the best answer.

How Wild Animals Became Tame

There was once a rich miller who was about to be married. He invited everyone to the wedding—even the wild animals in the forest. All the animals were flattered to be invited, so they all planned to attend.

On the day of the wedding, the fox was the first to leave the forest. Before he reached the miller's house, he bumped into a young boy on the road.

"Where are you going?" the young boy asked the fox.

"I'm going to the miller's wedding," the fox replied.

"Oh, no, you mustn't do that!" the boy answered in distress. "If you do, the miller will put you in a cage and make you catch mice for the rest of your life!"

The fox preferred his freedom, so he went back into the forest.

Soon after that, a bear lumbered by. The boy asked him if he was going to the miller's wedding.

"Of course," the bear answered proudly. "I wouldn't miss it for the world."

The boy begged, "You mustn't do that. The miller will see your beautiful coat and want it for a winter robe."

The bear was frightened by the boy's warning and returned to the forest.

Just then a white stallion pranced by on its way to the wedding.

"Don't go to the wedding," the boy warned the horse. "The miller will harness you and make you work for him. You will have to pull wagons and heavy loads."

"Don't be ridiculous," the horse responded, "I am too strong for any men to capture. If they put a rope on me, I'll just break loose and return to the forest."

"Men are stronger than you," the boy warned.

The horse laughed and said, "You are just jealous that you were not invited to the wedding. You do not want me to enjoy myself, but your little scheme is not working!"

So the white horse went to the wedding, where he was promptly caught and put into a stall. He was never again allowed to run free. Each day he hauled heavy loads of grain for the miller.

None of the wild animals that went to the miller's wedding ever came back to the forest. Since that day, they have had to obey the humans who tamed them.

1. What is the main problem in this story?

   Ⓐ The boy is not invited to the miller's wedding.

   Ⓑ Animals are invited to a wedding so they can be captured.

   Ⓒ The fox and bear decide not to attend the wedding.

   Ⓓ A white horse pulls a wagon filled with grain for the miller.

2. How is the white horse different from the fox and the bear?

   Ⓐ He is not invited to the wedding.

   Ⓑ He returns to the forest.

   Ⓒ He wants to work for the miller.

   Ⓓ He does not take the boy's advice.

3. Which words best describe the miller in this story?

   Ⓐ sneaky, dishonest

   Ⓑ caring, rich

   Ⓒ wise, hardworking

   Ⓓ silly, foolish

4. What is the theme of this story?

   Ⓐ You can't trust a miller.

   Ⓑ If you work hard, you will be rewarded.

   Ⓒ Good things come to those who wait.

   Ⓓ Be wary of people who flatter you.

GO ON

Read this passage. Then answer questions 5–8 by filling in the circle next to the best answer.

The Underground Army

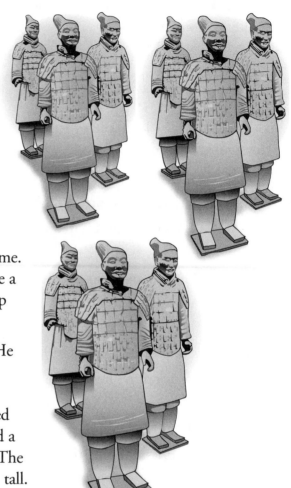

In 1974, some farmers in China were digging a well. As they drilled into the soil, they hit something unusual. It was an entire army of clay soldiers and horses! There were more than 8,000 life-size figures buried in the ground.

This hidden army was created more than 2,000 years ago to protect the Emperor of Qin. The emperor ruled all of China at the time. He believed that when he died, he would have a new life. An army of soldiers was made to help him rule another empire in his next life.

The Emperor of Qin was very powerful. He brought many parts of China together for the first time and became very wealthy. When he decided to build a tomb for himself, he wanted something big. He ordered his people to build a grand tomb with a palace, houses, and walls. The tomb itself was a pyramid more than 200 feet tall.

The emperor also ordered his people to build the army. All of the figures were made of terracotta, which is a kind of red clay. The clay was shaped into soldiers and horses, and then baked in ovens to harden. Real weapons and armor were added afterward, and the figures were painted to look real.

Soldiers in this army are arranged by rank, and every soldier is different. The figures vary in height and types of uniforms, and soldiers of different ranks have different hairstyles. The tallest soldiers are the generals. They stand in the front rows. Officers and foot soldiers stand in rows behind the generals.

Emperor Qin died in 210 B.C. and was buried in his tomb. Rare jewels, coins, and many other riches were buried with him. A map of the stars was made with pearls in the ceiling of the tomb, and a map of China lies on the tiled floor. In all, the emperor's compound covers more than three square miles. More than 700,000 laborers worked on the buildings and the terracotta army, and the project took 38 years to complete.

5. The farmers found the terracotta army in 1974 when they were—

Ⓐ building a pyramid.

Ⓑ digging a well.

Ⓒ looking for coins.

Ⓓ planting crops.

6. Emperor Qin built the army of clay soldiers to—

Ⓐ protect him in his next life.

Ⓑ guard the riches he owned.

Ⓒ trick his enemies.

Ⓓ give his people jobs.

7. In the terracotta army, why are the generals tallest?

Ⓐ They stand in the front row.

Ⓑ They have different hairstyles.

Ⓒ They are the most important soldiers.

Ⓓ They are part of the emperor's family.

8. What is this passage mostly about?

Ⓐ farming in China

Ⓑ the history of China

Ⓒ how to make terracotta

Ⓓ an army of clay figures

GO ON

Read this passage. Then answer questions 9–14 by filling in the circle next to the best answer.

The School Dance

Last week my life was a roller-coaster ride. There were lots of ups and downs, mainly because I was waiting for Paul Nunez to invite me to the school dance.

Actually, on Monday, I wasn't waiting for anything because I wasn't even planning to go to the dance. The one in September had not been great, and hardly anyone danced.

Then on Tuesday, my friend Lucille passed me a note in class. The note said, *Don't look now, Olivia, but Paul Nunez is looking at you.* I checked, and sure enough he was. The note continued, *Wouldn't it be awesome if he asked you to the dance?* I smiled at Lucille and nodded.

In math class on Wednesday, Lucille passed me a note that said, *I told Paul that you'd like to go to the dance with him. He said he'll ask you soon!* I stole a glance at Paul and caught him making eyes at me again. I tried to get back to the problems in my math book, but I couldn't seem to concentrate.

On Thursday, Lucille passed me a note during science. *So did he ask you yet?????* I shook my head slowly. A minute later, Lucille passed me another note. *I'll talk to Paul and find out what's going on!*

When the telephone rang on Thursday night, my heart started racing. But the caller wasn't Paul; it was Lucille.

"Apparently, Paul can't get up the nerve to invite you to the dance face to face," Lucille explained. "He wants me to tell him your e-mail address. Should I give it to him?"

I never thought I could make anyone feel nervous, but I guess I did. As I tried to go back to doing my homework, I wondered what would happen next.

A few minutes later, an e-mail came through, and sure enough, it was from Paul.

Hello, Olivia. I was wondering, if you're not doing anything on Saturday night, would you go to the school dance with me?

I clicked REPLY and typed *Hi, Paul! What a nice surprise! Yes, I'll go to the dance with you!* Then I took a deep breath and clicked SEND.

9. Where does most of this story take place?

    Ⓐ at Olivia's house

    Ⓑ at school

    Ⓒ at Paul's house

    Ⓓ on a roller coaster

10. In this story, Olivia and Lucille share information mostly by—

    Ⓐ talking on the phone.

    Ⓑ passing notes in class.

    Ⓒ sending e-mails.

    Ⓓ talking face to face.

11. What is Paul's main problem in this story?

    Ⓐ He does not understand his homework.

    Ⓑ He is not a very good dancer.

    Ⓒ He does not know Olivia's e-mail address.

    Ⓓ He is too nervous to talk to Olivia.

12. Which of these events happened *last*?

    Ⓐ Olivia noticed Paul Nunez looking at her.

    Ⓑ Lucille agreed to go to the dance with Paul.

    Ⓒ Paul asked Lucille for Olivia's e-mail address.

    Ⓓ Lucille passed a note to Olivia during science.

GO ON

13. For most of this story, Olivia has a hard time trying to—

Ⓐ concentrate on school work.

Ⓑ get along with Lucille.

Ⓒ use a computer keyboard.

Ⓓ learn how to dance.

14. Which word best describes Paul in this story?

Ⓐ foolish

Ⓑ lazy

Ⓒ shy

Ⓓ dishonest

Read this passage. Then answer questions 15–20 by filling in the circle next to the best answer.

The Right to Vote

Most young people assume that when they reach the age of 18, they will be able to vote in elections. As Americans, we think of voting as a right. But the right to vote hasn't always been so freely given.

When the United States was a young nation in 1800, the only people allowed to vote were white males over the age of 21. But not all white men could vote—only those who owned land.

Over the next 200 years, more and more people were allowed to vote. After the Civil War in the 1860s, African Americans gained the right to vote. However, there were many restrictions. For example, a voter had to be able to read and write. Most African Americans at that time were former slaves who never went to school. They had never learned to read. Also, some places made voters pay poll taxes before they voted. For most former slaves who had no money, the poll taxes were not affordable. So they could not cast their votes.

Women did not win the right to vote until 1920. In the late 1800s, many women protested by marching in parades. Both men and women wrote newspaper articles supporting women's right to vote. Finally, a majority of Americans decided that women should have the right to vote, too. Congress passed the 19th Amendment to the Constitution because of the change in public opinion.

In 1965, African Americans led by Martin Luther King, Jr., began demonstrating to protect their voting rights. Even though the law said they had the right to vote, African Americans were often turned away from polling places. In 1965, President Lyndon Johnson signed the Voting Rights Act. This law made it illegal to stop African Americans from voting.

In 1971, the country was involved in a war in Vietnam. Young people were drafted at the age of 18 and sent to war, but they still couldn't vote until they were 21. Many Americans protested this unfairness. They asked Congress why 18-year-olds were old enough to fight but not old enough to vote. In response, Congress passed the 26th Amendment, which lowered the voting age from 21 to 18.

New voting laws are passed when a need arises. When enough people demand their rights, the laws get changed.

GO ON

15. How were U.S. voting laws in 1800 different from voting laws of today?

(A) Voters in 1800 had to prove they could read.

(B) Only white men who owned land could vote in 1800.

(C) In 1800, any citizen over 21 could vote.

(D) Men could vote at age 18, but women could not.

16. Congress gave women the right to vote in 1920 because—

(A) most women could read and write.

(B) women had the money to pay the poll tax.

(C) African Americans began demonstrating.

(D) a majority of Americans demanded it.

17. Just after the Civil War, why were many African Americans unable to vote?

(A) They did not own enough land.

(B) The law said that African Americans could not vote.

(C) The polling places were too far from their homes.

(D) They could not read or write.

18. Congress changed the voting laws in 1971 by—

(A) lowering the voting age to 18.

(B) allowing women to vote.

(C) raising the poll tax charged to voters.

(D) letting African Americans vote.

19. In 1965, President Johnson signed a law to—

Ⓐ stop people from demonstrating.

Ⓑ draft young people into the army.

Ⓒ protect African Americans' voting rights.

Ⓓ give women the right to vote.

20. Which sentence best summarizes the passage?

Ⓐ Only white men who owned land were allowed to vote in elections.

Ⓑ Voting rights in the United States have changed several times since 1800.

Ⓒ Women were not allowed to vote in elections until 1920.

Ⓓ Young people in the United States were drafted into the army at the age of 18.

GO ON

Vocabulary/Word Study

Read each question and choose the best answer. Fill in the circle next to the answer you choose.

21. The miller will see the bear's beautiful coat and want it for a winter robe.
    What is the meaning of *coat* in this sentence?
    Ⓐ an outer garment to keep a person warm
    Ⓑ a layer of something such as paint
    Ⓒ fur that covers an animal
    Ⓓ to cover something

22. It was an army of clay soldiers.
    Which is the correct plural form of *army*?
    Ⓐ armies   Ⓒ armyes
    Ⓑ armys   Ⓓ armyses

23. Over the next 200 years, more people were allowed to vote.
    Which word is a synonym for *allowed*?
    Ⓐ permitted   Ⓒ supposed
    Ⓑ refused   Ⓓ reminded

24. For most former slaves who had no money, the poll taxes were not affordable.
    In this sentence, the word *affordable* means—
    Ⓐ one who pays.   Ⓒ not paid.
    Ⓑ able to be paid. Ⓓ paid again.

25. The Emperor of Qin was very powerful.
    Which word is an antonym for *powerful*?
    Ⓐ strong   Ⓒ weak
    Ⓑ clever   Ⓓ important

26. A man checked our tickets and inspected our bags at the airport.

The word *inspected* contains the Latin root *spec*, meaning—

Ⓐ take.

Ⓑ see.

Ⓒ fix.

Ⓓ open.

27. In which sentence is the word *waist* used correctly?

Ⓐ Don't <u>waist</u> too much time.

Ⓑ Plastic containers produce a lot of <u>waist</u>.

Ⓒ Put the belt around your <u>waist</u>.

Ⓓ If you <u>waist</u> your money, you'll be sorry.

28. A light appeared in the window.

Which word is *not* in the same word family as *appeared*?

Ⓐ reappear   Ⓒ disappear

Ⓑ appearance   Ⓓ wrapper

29. A dictionary page has the guide words *dew/dice*.

Which word would be found on the same page?

Ⓐ develop   Ⓒ diamond

Ⓑ different   Ⓓ dining

30. Last month, Mr. Marley _____ more than 100 books to the library.

Which verb form best fits in this sentence?

Ⓐ donate   Ⓒ donating

Ⓑ donates   Ⓓ donated

GO ON

Grammar, Usage, and Mechanics

The following is the rough draft of a student's story. It contains errors. Read the draft. Then read each question and decide which is the best answer. Fill in the circle next to the answer you choose.

My Best Friend and Her Dog

(1) Jenni and I are best friends, which is lucky for me. (2) Really like sports. (3) It's also lucky because I spend afternoons at her house while my dad works. (4) Being at Jenni's house is great because she has the best video games. (5) Then one day she told me she wanted a dog.

(6) "Why don't you get a kitten?" I asked her. (7) I haven't never been that crazy about dogs, but I love kittens. (8) The truth is that dogs scare me, but I didn't want to admit it. (9) Jenni <u>clear</u> didn't want a cat, though, so I started talking about other great pets.

(10) Gerbils are really neat! I told Jenni one day. (11) A few days later, I mentioned that teaching a parrot how to talk would be really fun. (12) But nothing I said or did could change my friend's mind. (13) She really wanted a dog. (14) Eventually, her parents took her to pick out a puppy.

(15) Jenni chose a little dog with curly brown hair, and she named him Sport. (16) Sport was a cockapoo—part poodle and part cocker spaniel. (17) Jenni thought he was the cutest puppy in the world, and he *was* cute to look at. (18) But I hated the way he got all excited and barked and jumped and scratched my legs every time I came to the house. (19) I couldn't make him stop, and neither could Jenni. (20) It really bugged me!

31. How can sentence 2 be written correctly?

Ⓐ Really like playing all kinds of sports.

Ⓑ We both really like sports.

Ⓒ Like sports and her a real lot.

Ⓓ Leave as is.

32. What is the correct way to write sentence 7?

Ⓐ I have not never been that crazy about dogs, but I love kittens.

Ⓑ I have never been that crazy about dogs, but I love kittens.

Ⓒ I haven't not ever been that crazy about dogs, but I love kittens.

Ⓓ Leave as is.

33. What is the correct way to write the underlined word in sentence 9?

Ⓐ clearer

Ⓑ clearest

Ⓒ clearly

Ⓓ Leave as is.

34. What is the correct way to write sentence 10?

Ⓐ "Gerbils are really neat!" I told Jenni one day.

Ⓑ "Gerbils are really neat! I told Jenni one day."

Ⓒ Gerbils are really neat! "I told Jenni one day."

Ⓓ Leave as is.

35. How can sentences 12 and 13 best be combined?

Ⓐ But nothing I said or did could change my friend's mind, although she really wanted a dog.

Ⓑ But nothing I said or did could change my friend's mind, or she really wanted a dog.

Ⓒ But nothing I said or did could change my friend's mind, and she really wanted a dog.

Ⓓ But nothing I said or did could change my friend's mind because she really wanted a dog.

GO ON

The following is the rough draft of a student's report. It contains errors. Read the draft. Then read each question and decide which is the best answer. Fill in the circle next to the answer you choose.

Confused about Crocodilians?

(1) Can you tell the difference between alligators and crocodiles? (2) For a long time, I could not tell them apart. (3) Their many similarities were really confusing to I. (4) They are similar in shape, and they both live in or near water. (5) Both belong to a group of animals called "crocodilians." (6) In addition, both live in the wild, have big teeth, and can be dangerous to people.

(7) Yet alligators and crocodiles have differences, too. (8) With a few facts, you can learn to tell them apart. (9) There are four things to check.

(10) First, look at the animal's color. (11) Alligators are dark-colored, either black or a very dark gray. (12) Crocodiles are lighter. (13) A greenish brown or sandy color.

(14) Next, observe the animal's snout. (15) An alligator's snout is wide and rounded or U-shaped. (16) In contrast, a crocodile's snout is <u>longest and more pointed</u>.

(17) When the animal closes its mouth, notice the teeth. (18) Only the upper teeth show when an <u>alligator's</u> jaw is closed. (19) The lower teeth are hidden. (20) If you see any of the lower teeth, you can be sure the animal is a crocodile.

(21) Last, consider the animal's habitat. (22) Alligators usually live in fresh water habitats, crocodiles live in saltwater. (23) Remember these points, and you will never get confused about crocodilians again.

36. What is the correct way to write sentence 3?

Ⓐ Their many similarities were really confusing to me.

Ⓑ Their many similarities were really confusing to it.

Ⓒ Their many similarities were really confusing to he.

Ⓓ Leave as is.

37. Which numbered sentence is a sentence fragment?

Ⓐ sentence 10

Ⓑ sentence 11

Ⓒ sentence 12

Ⓓ sentence 13

38. What is the correct way to write the underlined part of sentence 16?

Ⓐ longer and more pointed

Ⓑ longest and pointedest

Ⓒ longest and most pointed

Ⓓ Leave as is.

39. What is the correct way to write the underlined word in sentence 18?

Ⓐ alligators

Ⓑ alligators'

Ⓒ alligators's

Ⓓ Leave as is.

40. How should sentence 22 be written correctly?

Ⓐ Alligators usually live in fresh water habitats; as a result, crocodiles live in saltwater.

Ⓑ Alligators usually live in fresh water habitats, while crocodiles live in saltwater.

Ⓒ Alligators usually live in fresh water habitats because crocodiles live in saltwater.

Ⓓ Leave as is.

GO ON

Writing

Read the prompt. Write your essay on the lines below and on the next page, or on the answer document.

Write a personal narrative telling about a time when something unexpected happened to you.

When you write your personal narrative, remember to
- tell what happened in order,
- include descriptive language and sensory details to make your narrative interesting, and
- use correct grammar, spelling, punctuation, and capitalization.

_____

_____

_____

_____

_____

_____

_____

_____

_____

Listening

Listen to each passage as your teacher reads it aloud. Then listen to the questions. Choose the best answer to each question. Fill in the circle beside the answer you choose.

41.
Ⓐ Kim's dad drove her to the mall.
Ⓑ Lizzie said she didn't want to go shopping.
Ⓒ Kim checked her list of school supplies.
Ⓓ Lizzie told some jokes to make Kim laugh.

42.
Ⓐ at a shopping mall
Ⓑ at school
Ⓒ at Kim's house
Ⓓ at Lizzie's house

43.
Ⓐ She could not decide which color binder to buy.
Ⓑ Risa was telling her what things to choose.
Ⓒ Lizzie did not want to be friends with her anymore.
Ⓓ She did not like shopping for school supplies.

44.
Ⓐ Risa gave Kim a new green binder.
Ⓑ Kim called Lizzie on the phone.
Ⓒ Lizzie met Kim at the Super Mart.
Ⓓ Kim saw Risa at the Super Mart.

45.
Ⓐ They got school supplies and had lunch.
Ⓑ They got a ride home with Kim's dad.
Ⓒ They met Lizzie at a restaurant in the mall.
Ⓓ They went to a movie at the shopping mall.

46.
Ⓐ how volleyball is played

Ⓑ a YMCA in Massachusetts

Ⓒ how volleyball was invented

Ⓓ William Morgan's career

47.
Ⓐ He wanted to find a team sport for older men.

Ⓑ He was tired of playing basketball.

Ⓒ He didn't have equipment for other games.

Ⓓ He wanted to go to the Olympics.

48.
Ⓐ It was a slower, gentler game.

Ⓑ It had smaller teams.

Ⓒ It wasn't as much fun.

Ⓓ It took less time to play.

49.
Ⓐ Schools did not have to buy any equipment.

Ⓑ It could be played indoors or outdoors.

Ⓒ The game did not require players to use rackets.

Ⓓ Both boys and girls could play it.

50.
Ⓐ Basketball and volleyball are both team sports that use nets.

Ⓑ In 1895, William Morgan was the director of a YMCA in Massachusetts.

Ⓒ Today, volleyball is a popular team sport in America and is played by both boys and girls.

Ⓓ Since 1895, volleyball has become a fast, popular sport played all over the world.

rSkills® Test Answer Document Test _____

Name _____ Date _____

Multiple-Choice Questions

1.	Ⓐ	Ⓑ	Ⓒ	Ⓓ	16.	Ⓐ	Ⓑ	Ⓒ	Ⓓ
2.	Ⓐ	Ⓑ	Ⓒ	Ⓓ	17.	Ⓐ	Ⓑ	Ⓒ	Ⓓ
3.	Ⓐ	Ⓑ	Ⓒ	Ⓓ	18.	Ⓐ	Ⓑ	Ⓒ	Ⓓ
4.	Ⓐ	Ⓑ	Ⓒ	Ⓓ	19.	Ⓐ	Ⓑ	Ⓒ	Ⓓ
5.	Ⓐ	Ⓑ	Ⓒ	Ⓓ	20.	Ⓐ	Ⓑ	Ⓒ	Ⓓ
6.	Ⓐ	Ⓑ	Ⓒ	Ⓓ	21.	Ⓐ	Ⓑ	Ⓒ	Ⓓ
7.	Ⓐ	Ⓑ	Ⓒ	Ⓓ	22.	Ⓐ	Ⓑ	Ⓒ	Ⓓ
8.	Ⓐ	Ⓑ	Ⓒ	Ⓓ	23.	Ⓐ	Ⓑ	Ⓒ	Ⓓ
9.	Ⓐ	Ⓑ	Ⓒ	Ⓓ	24.	Ⓐ	Ⓑ	Ⓒ	Ⓓ
10.	Ⓐ	Ⓑ	Ⓒ	Ⓓ	25.	Ⓐ	Ⓑ	Ⓒ	Ⓓ
11.	Ⓐ	Ⓑ	Ⓒ	Ⓓ	26.	Ⓐ	Ⓑ	Ⓒ	Ⓓ
12.	Ⓐ	Ⓑ	Ⓒ	Ⓓ	27.	Ⓐ	Ⓑ	Ⓒ	Ⓓ
13.	Ⓐ	Ⓑ	Ⓒ	Ⓓ	28.	Ⓐ	Ⓑ	Ⓒ	Ⓓ
14.	Ⓐ	Ⓑ	Ⓒ	Ⓓ	29.	Ⓐ	Ⓑ	Ⓒ	Ⓓ
15.	Ⓐ	Ⓑ	Ⓒ	Ⓓ	30.	Ⓐ	Ⓑ	Ⓒ	Ⓓ

Open-Response Questions

31. _____

_____

_____

_____

_____

Name _____ Date _____

Open-Response Questions *(continued)*

32. _____

_____

_____

_____

_____

Writing

_____

_____

_____

_____

_____

_____

_____

_____

_____

_____

_____

rSkills® Midyear/End-of-Year Test Answer Document

Name _____   Test _____

Comprehension

1. Ⓐ Ⓑ Ⓒ Ⓓ
2. Ⓐ Ⓑ Ⓒ Ⓓ
3. Ⓐ Ⓑ Ⓒ Ⓓ
4. Ⓐ Ⓑ Ⓒ Ⓓ
5. Ⓐ Ⓑ Ⓒ Ⓓ
6. Ⓐ Ⓑ Ⓒ Ⓓ
7. Ⓐ Ⓑ Ⓒ Ⓓ
8. Ⓐ Ⓑ Ⓒ Ⓓ
9. Ⓐ Ⓑ Ⓒ Ⓓ
10. Ⓐ Ⓑ Ⓒ Ⓓ
11. Ⓐ Ⓑ Ⓒ Ⓓ
12. Ⓐ Ⓑ Ⓒ Ⓓ
13. Ⓐ Ⓑ Ⓒ Ⓓ
14. Ⓐ Ⓑ Ⓒ Ⓓ
15. Ⓐ Ⓑ Ⓒ Ⓓ
16. Ⓐ Ⓑ Ⓒ Ⓓ
17. Ⓐ Ⓑ Ⓒ Ⓓ
18. Ⓐ Ⓑ Ⓒ Ⓓ
19. Ⓐ Ⓑ Ⓒ Ⓓ
20. Ⓐ Ⓑ Ⓒ Ⓓ

Vocabulary/Word Study

21. Ⓐ Ⓑ Ⓒ Ⓓ
22. Ⓐ Ⓑ Ⓒ Ⓓ
23. Ⓐ Ⓑ Ⓒ Ⓓ
24. Ⓐ Ⓑ Ⓒ Ⓓ
25. Ⓐ Ⓑ Ⓒ Ⓓ
26. Ⓐ Ⓑ Ⓒ Ⓓ
27. Ⓐ Ⓑ Ⓒ Ⓓ
28. Ⓐ Ⓑ Ⓒ Ⓓ
29. Ⓐ Ⓑ Ⓒ Ⓓ
30. Ⓐ Ⓑ Ⓒ Ⓓ

Grammar, Usage, and Mechanics

31. Ⓐ Ⓑ Ⓒ Ⓓ
32. Ⓐ Ⓑ Ⓒ Ⓓ
33. Ⓐ Ⓑ Ⓒ Ⓓ
34. Ⓐ Ⓑ Ⓒ Ⓓ
35. Ⓐ Ⓑ Ⓒ Ⓓ
36. Ⓐ Ⓑ Ⓒ Ⓓ
37. Ⓐ Ⓑ Ⓒ Ⓓ
38. Ⓐ Ⓑ Ⓒ Ⓓ
39. Ⓐ Ⓑ Ⓒ Ⓓ
40. Ⓐ Ⓑ Ⓒ Ⓓ

Listening

41. Ⓐ Ⓑ Ⓒ Ⓓ
42. Ⓐ Ⓑ Ⓒ Ⓓ
43. Ⓐ Ⓑ Ⓒ Ⓓ
44. Ⓐ Ⓑ Ⓒ Ⓓ
45. Ⓐ Ⓑ Ⓒ Ⓓ
46. Ⓐ Ⓑ Ⓒ Ⓓ
47. Ⓐ Ⓑ Ⓒ Ⓓ
48. Ⓐ Ⓑ Ⓒ Ⓓ
49. Ⓐ Ⓑ Ⓒ Ⓓ
50. Ⓐ Ⓑ Ⓒ Ⓓ

rSkills® Midyear/End-of-Year Test Answer Document

Name _____

Writing   **page** _____

_____

_____

_____

_____

_____

_____

_____

_____

_____

_____

_____

_____

_____

_____

Test 1a Answer Key

Sample Questions

Sample **A.** B

Sample **B.** D

Comprehension

1.	B	(Main Idea and Details)
2.	C	(Sequence of Events)
3.	B	(Main Idea and Details)
4.	D	(Sequence of Events)
5.	A	(Main Idea and Details)
6.	C	(Sequence of Events)
7.	C	(Main Idea and Details)
8.	D	(Main Idea and Details)
9.	A	(Sequence of Events)
10.	D	(Main Idea and Details)

Vocabulary/Word Study

11.	B	(Prefixes)
12.	C	(Prefixes)
13.	B	(Suffixes)
14.	D	(Synonyms)
15.	A	(Antonyms)
16.	D	(Antonyms)

Vocabulary/Word Study (continued)

17.	C	(Suffixes)
18.	B	(Synonyms)
19.	A	(Synonyms)
20.	C	(Suffixes)

Grammar, Usage, and Mechanics

21.	C	(Identifying Sentences and Fragments)
22.	B	(Using End Punctuation)
23.	B	(Correcting Sentence Fragments)
24.	A	(Using Capitals)
25.	B	(Identifying Sentences and Fragments)
26.	D	(Using End Punctuation)
27.	A	(Correcting Sentence Fragments)
28.	C	(Using Capitals)
29.	A	(Identifying Simple and Compound Sentences)
30.	B	(Identifying Simple and Compound Sentences)

Open Response (sample answers)

31. The wind spread the fire to a canyon. The fire got out of control.

32. The trees were cut down to make fields for farmers.

Writing

Use the scoring rubric on page 19 and the criteria for expository writing on page 20 to evaluate students' written responses.

Test 2a Answer Key

Sample Questions

Sample A. A

Sample B. C

Comprehension

1.	D	(Summarize)
2.	A	(Sequence of Events)
3.	D	(Summarize)
4.	A	(Main Idea and Details)
5.	B	(Summarize)
6.	B	(Plot)
7.	B	(Character)
8.	D	(Setting)
9.	C	(Plot)
10.	D	(Plot)

Vocabulary/Word Study

11.	B	(Word Families)
12.	A	(Homophones)
13.	A	(Context Clues)
14.	D	(Context Clues)
15.	C	(Compound Words)

Vocabulary/Word Study (continued)

16.	B	(Compound Words)
17.	B	(Word Families)
18.	D	(Homophones)
19.	C	(Context Clues)
20.	A	(Compound Words)

Grammar, Usage, and Mechanics

21.	D	(Correcting Run-On Sentences)
22.	C	(Using Correct Verb Tense)
23.	A	(Using Correct Word Order)
24.	C	(Using Commas in a Series)
25.	B	(Correcting Run-On Sentences)
26.	D	(Using Correct Word Order)
27.	C	(Using Correct Verb Tense)
28.	A	(Using Commas in a Series)
29.	D	(Combining Sentences)
30.	B	(Combining Sentences)

Open Response (sample answers)

31. Students work together on a team. This helps them get to know each other better so they won't fight.

32. Mr. Anson is in a barn. There are cows to milk and chickens that lay eggs.

Writing

Use the scoring rubric on page 19 and the criteria for response to literature writing on page 21 to evaluate students' written responses.

Test 3a Answer Key

Sample Questions

Sample **A.** C

Sample **B.** B

Comprehension

1. D (Summarize)
2. C (Problem and Solution)
3. D (Problem and Solution)
4. B (Problem and Solution)
5. C (Theme)
6. A (Plot)
7. C (Character)
8. A (Character)
9. D (Setting)
10. B (Character)

Vocabulary/Word Study

11. B (Homophones)
12. C (Homophones)
13. A (Idioms)
14. D (Idioms)
15. C (Word Families)
16. B (Multiple-Meaning Words)

Vocabulary/Word Study (continued)

17. B (Homophones)
18. A (Idioms)
19. B (Word Families)
20. D (Multiple-Meaning Words)

Grammar, Usage, and Mechanics

21. A (Using Irregular Verbs)
22. B (Using Commas With Introductory Words)
23. C (Subject-Verb Agreement)
24. B (Using Possessives)
25. D (Using Irregular Verbs)
26. C (Using Commas With Introductory Words)
27. B (Subject-Verb Agreement)
28. D (Using Possessives)
29. C (Using Conjunctions)
30. A (Using Conjunctions)

Open Response (sample answers)

31. Many Egyptian children died soon after birth. Some were poor and started working as early as age four.

32. I think Diana felt happy to be able to walk again.

Writing

Use the scoring rubric on page 19 and the criteria for persuasive writing on page 21 to evaluate students' written responses.

Test 4a Answer Key

Sample Questions

Sample A. C

Sample B. D

Comprehension

1. C (Summarize)

2. B (Cause and Effect)

3. C (Cause and Effect)

4. A (Compare and Contrast)

5. C (Cause and Effect)

6. B (Cause and Effect)

7. D (Compare and Contrast)

8. A (Problem and Solution)

9. D (Problem and Solution)

10. D (Compare and Contrast)

Vocabulary/Word Study

11. B (Synonyms)

12. A (Multiple-Meaning Words)

13. C (Verb Endings)

14. B (Verb Endings)

15. D (Suffixes)

Vocabulary/Word Study (continued)

16. A (Using a Dictionary)

17. A (Synonyms)

18. C (Multiple-Meaning Words)

19. D (Suffixes)

20. B (Using a Dictionary)

Grammar, Usage, and Mechanics

21. B (Using Subject and Object Pronouns)

22. C (Avoiding Double Negatives)

23. D (Using Adjectives That Compare)

24. A (Using Quotation Marks)

25. D (Using Subject and Object Pronouns)

26. A (Avoiding Double Negatives)

27. D (Using Adjectives That Compare)

28. B (Using Quotation Marks)

29. C (Using Compound Sentences)

30. B (Using Compound Sentences)

Open Response (sample answers)

31. The animals that live in a park are different from those in a zoo. A zoo may have animals that are rare.

32. Alice Waters's garden is used to teach children about growing and eating good food.

Writing

Use the scoring rubric on page 19 and the criteria for descriptive writing on page 21 to evaluate students' written responses.

Test 5a Answer Key

Sample Questions

Sample **A.** B
Sample **B.** A

Comprehension

1. A (Make Inferences)
2. B (Compare and Contrast)
3. C (Cause and Effect)
4. C (Compare and Contrast)
5. A (Make Inferences)
6. D (Setting)
7. B (Plot)
8. C (Character)
9. D (Make Inferences)
10. D (Theme)

Vocabulary/Word Study

11. B (Antonyms)
12. A (Noun Endings)
13. C (Noun Endings)
14. C (Using a Dictionary)
15. A (Using a Dictionary)

Vocabulary/Word Study (continued)

16. B (Multiple-Meaning Words)
17. D (Antonyms)
18. B (Noun Endings)
19. A (Using a Dictionary)
20. D (Multiple-Meaning Words)

Grammar, Usage, and Mechanics

21. D (Identifying Sentences and Fragments)
22. C (Correcting Sentence Fragments)
23. A (Using Adverbs)
24. B (Using Adverbs)
25. C (Identifying Sentences and Fragments)
26. D (Correcting Sentence Fragments)
27. C (Using Adverbs)
28. D (Identifying Simple and Compound Sentences)
29. A (Combining Sentences)
30. B (Combining Sentences)

Open Response (sample answers)

31. I think the women Elizabeth Blackwell helped liked and respected her. Elizabeth helped them feel better. She made it easier for other women to become doctors.

32. Roy helped Tanisha by holding her hand. He also waited outside her class to make sure she was okay.

Writing

Use the scoring rubric on page 19 and the criteria for narrative writing on page 20 to evaluate students' written responses.

Test 1b Answer Key

Sample Questions

Sample **A.** C

Sample **B.** B

Comprehension

1.	A	(Main Idea and Details)
2.	C	(Sequence of Events)
3.	A	(Main Idea and Details)
4.	B	(Sequence of Events)
5.	B	(Main Idea and Details)
6.	D	(Main Idea and Details)
7.	A	(Sequence of Events)
8.	D	(Main Idea and Details)
9.	C	(Sequence of Events)
10.	B	(Main Idea and Details)

Vocabulary/Word Study

11.	C	(Prefixes)
12.	A	(Prefixes)
13.	B	(Suffixes)
14.	C	(Synonyms)
15.	D	(Antonyms)

Vocabulary/Word Study *(continued)*

16.	C	(Antonyms)
17.	A	(Suffixes)
18.	D	(Synonyms)
19.	B	(Synonyms)
20.	A	(Suffixes)

Grammar, Usage, and Mechanics

21.	B	(Identifying Sentences and Fragments)
22.	B	(Using End Punctuation)
23.	A	(Correcting Sentence Fragments)
24.	D	(Using Capitals)
25.	D	(Identifying Sentences and Fragments)
26.	B	(Using End Punctuation)
27.	B	(Correcting Sentence Fragments)
28.	A	(Using Capitals)
29.	A	(Identifying Simple and Compound Sentences)
30.	C	(Identifying Simple and Compound Sentences)

Open Response (sample answers)

31. The animals didn't panic. Instead, big animals moved ahead of the flames to safe areas. Small animals burrowed underground.

32. The family hurried to their room. They gathered up their suitcases and documents. Then they went through the ship to the gangway.

Writing

Use the scoring rubric on page 19 and the criteria for expository writing on page 20 to evaluate students' written responses.

Test 2b Answer Key

Sample Questions

Sample A. D
Sample B. B

Comprehension

1.	B	(Main Idea and Details)
2.	D	(Sequence of Events)
3.	A	(Summarize)
4.	C	(Summarize)
5.	C	(Summarize)
6.	D	(Setting)
7.	A	(Character)
8.	A	(Plot)
9.	C	(Plot)
10.	C	(Setting)

Vocabulary/Word Study

11.	D	(Word Families)
12.	B	(Homophones)
13.	D	(Context Clues)
14.	B	(Context Clues)
15.	A	(Compound Words)

Vocabulary/Word Study (continued)

16.	C	(Compound Words)
17.	B	(Word Families)
18.	A	(Homophones)
19.	C	(Context Clues)
20.	D	(Compound Words)

Grammar, Usage, and Mechanics

21.	A	(Correcting Run-On Sentences)
22.	D	(Using Correct Verb Tense)
23.	B	(Using Correct Word Order)
24.	D	(Using Commas in a Series)
25.	A	(Correcting Run-On Sentences)
26.	A	(Using Correct Word Order)
27.	C	(Using Correct Verb Tense)
28.	B	(Using Commas in a Series)
29.	C	(Combining Sentences)
30.	A	(Combining Sentences)

Open Response (sample answers)

31. Cliques only let certain people join. The students in a clique can be mean and hurt other students.

32. Adamana was barren. There was nothing except for a few buildings and a waiting bus.

Writing

Use the scoring rubric on page 19 and the criteria for response to literature writing on page 21 to evaluate students' written responses.

Test 3b Answer Key

Sample Questions

Sample **A.** B

Sample **B.** C

Comprehension

1. D (Problem and Solution)

2. D (Problem and Solution)

3. A (Problem and Solution)

4. A (Summarize)

5. D (Setting)

6. B (Plot)

7. D (Character)

8. C (Character)

9. C (Plot)

10. A (Theme)

Vocabulary/Word Study

11. B (Homophones)

12. C (Homophones)

13. B (Idioms)

14. D (Idioms)

15. A (Word Families)

16. C (Multiple-Meaning Words)

Vocabulary/Word Study *(continued)*

17. C (Homophones)

18. A (Idioms)

19. D (Word Families)

20. B (Multiple-Meaning Words)

Grammar, Usage, and Mechanics

21. B (Using Irregular Verbs)

22. D (Using Commas With Introductory Words)

23. C (Subject-Verb Agreement)

24. A (Using Possessives)

25. B (Using Irregular Verbs)

26. C (Using Commas With Introductory Words)

27. A (Subject-Verb Agreement)

28. D (Using Possessives)

29. B (Using Conjunctions)

30. A (Using Conjunctions)

Open Response (sample answers)

31. Some mummies are buried in ice. Global warming could melt the ice before the mummies are found. The mummies would decompose.

32. Eric tries hard and doesn't give up easily. He also has courage. He tries new things, like joining the swim team.

Writing

Use the scoring rubric on page 19 and the criteria for persuasive writing on page 21 to evaluate students' written responses.

Test 4b Answer Key

Sample Questions

Sample **A.** D

Sample **B.** B

Comprehension

1. B   (Problem and Solution)
2. D   (Cause and Effect)
3. A   (Cause and Effect)
4. B   (Summarize)
5. C   (Compare and Contrast)
6. B   (Cause and Effect)
7. C   (Problem and Solution)
8. D   (Cause and Effect)
9. C   (Compare and Contrast)
10. A   (Compare and Contrast)

Vocabulary/Word Study

11. A   (Synonyms)
12. D   (Multiple-Meaning Words)
13. C   (Verb Endings)
14. B   (Verb Endings)
15. C   (Suffixes)

Vocabulary/Word Study (continued)

16. D   (Using a Dictionary)
17. D   (Synonyms)
18. C   (Multiple-Meaning Words)
19. C   (Suffixes)
20. A   (Using a Dictionary)

Grammar, Usage, and Mechanics

21. B   (Using Subject and Object Pronouns)
22. D   (Avoiding Double Negatives)
23. C   (Using Adjectives That Compare)
24. B   (Using Quotation Marks)
25. B   (Using Subject and Object Pronouns)
26. A   (Avoiding Double Negatives)
27. B   (Using Adjectives That Compare)
28. D   (Using Quotation Marks)
29. B   (Using Compound Sentences)
30. D   (Using Compound Sentences)

Open Response (sample answers)

31. Animal rescuers release an animal in a place where it can find food and shelter. Elk are set free in the mountains in spring, when they can find plants to eat. Bears are set free near caves in late fall, right before they hibernate.

32. An athlete who eats too much will store fat and gain weight. An athlete who eats too little will lose muscle. Athletes need muscles to play a sport.

Writing

Use the scoring rubric on page 19 and the criteria for descriptive writing on page 21 to evaluate students' written responses.

Test 5b Answer Key

Sample Questions

Sample A. B

Sample B. A

Comprehension

1. A (Compare and Contrast)
2. C (Cause and Effect)
3. A (Compare and Contrast)
4. D (Make Inferences)
5. B (Make Inferences)
6. D (Character)
7. C (Setting)
8. A (Plot)
9. A (Make Inferences)
10. B (Theme)

Vocabulary/Word Study

11. A (Antonyms)
12. B (Noun Endings)
13. C (Noun Endings)
14. A (Using a Dictionary)
15. D (Using a Dictionary)
16. B (Multiple-Meaning Words)

Vocabulary/Word Study (continued)

17. A (Antonyms)
18. C (Noun Endings)
19. D (Using a Dictionary)
20. B (Multiple-Meaning Words)

Grammar, Usage, and Mechanics

21. A (Identifying Sentences and Fragments)
22. D (Correcting Sentence Fragments)
23. B (Using Adverbs)
24. C (Using Adverbs)
25. A (Identifying Sentences and Fragments)
26. D (Correcting Sentence Fragments)
27. B (Using Adverbs)
28. C (Identifying Simple and Compound Sentences)
29. B (Combining Sentences)
30. A (Combining Sentences)

Open Response (sample answers)

31. Benjamin Roberts felt that it was unfair to have separate schools for white and black children. He wanted his daughter, Sarah, to go to school with white children.

32. At the beginning of her diary, Kaitlyn seems scared and worried about living in a new place. At the end of her diary, Kaitlyn sounds happier. She talks about making a puppet and makes a joke about Jamal's puppet.

Writing

Use the scoring rubric on page 19 and the criteria for narrative writing on page 20 to evaluate students' written responses.

rSkills Midyear Test (Level a) Answer Key

Sample Questions

Sample **A.** A
Sample **B.** B

Comprehension

1. A (Setting)
2. C (Sequence of Events)
3. B (Character)
4. C (Plot)
5. D (Main Idea and Details)
6. B (Main Idea and Details)
7. B (Problem and Solution)
8. A (Summarize)
9. B (Setting)
10. C (Problem and Solution)
11. A (Sequence of Events)
12. D (Plot)
13. A (Character)
14. C (Character)
15. A (Summarize)
16. B (Sequence of Events)
17. D (Main Idea and Details)
18. D (Main Idea and Details)
19. C (Sequence of Events)
20. A (Summarize)

Vocabulary/Word Study

21. D (Synonyms)
22. B (Idioms)
23. C (Prefixes)
24. A (Antonyms)
25. D (Context Clues)
26. A (Homophones)
27. B (Homophones)
28. C (Word Families)

Vocabulary/Word Study (continued)

29. C (Compound Words)
30. A (Suffixes)

Grammar, Usage, and Mechanics

31. B (Identifying Sentences and Fragments)
32. C (Correcting Run-on Sentences)
33. B (Using Capitals)
34. C (Using Conjunctions)
35. A (Using Irregular Verbs)
36. A (Using Commas with Introductory Words)
37. B (Combining Sentences)
38. A (Using Correct Word Order)
39. C (Correcting Sentence Fragments)
40. D (Using Correct Verb Tense)

Writing

Use the scoring rubric on page 19 and the criteria for expository writing on page 20 to evaluate students' written responses.

Listening

41. B (Sequence of Events)
42. A (Character)
43. C (Plot)
44. C (Problem and Solution)
45. D (Setting)
46. C (Main Idea and Details)
47. D (Sequence of Events)
48. B (Main Idea and Details)
49. D (Problem and Solution)
50. A (Summarize)

rSkills End-of-Year Test (Level a) Answer Key

Sample Questions

Sample **A.** B

Sample **B.** D

Comprehension

1. B (Compare and Contrast)
2. D (Plot)
3. A (Character)
4. B (Theme)
5. A (Main Idea and Details)
6. C (Cause and Effect)
7. C (Compare and Contrast)
8. D (Summarize)
9. C (Sequence of Events)
10. D (Problem and Solution)
11. A (Setting)
12. D (Plot)
13. C (Make Inferences)
14. B (Character)
15. A (Compare and Contrast)
16. C (Cause and Effect)
17. D (Problem and Solution)
18. D (Problem and Solution)
19. A (Summarize)
20. B (Summarize)

Vocabulary/Word Study

21. C (Multiple-Meaning Words)
22. D (Synonyms)
23. B (Antonyms)
24. A (Noun Endings)
25. A (Context Clues)
26. C (Using a Dictionary)
27. D (Suffixes)
28. C (Word Families)

Vocabulary/Word Study *(continued)*

29. B (Verb Endings)
30. D (Latin and Greek Roots)

Grammar, Usage, and Mechanics

31. C (Using Subject and Object Pronouns)
32. B (Avoiding Double Negatives)
33. A (Using Quotation Marks)
34. D (Identifying Sentences and Fragments)
35. C (Using Adjectives That Compare)
36. D (Identifying Simple and Compound Sentences)
37. D (Using Adverbs)
38. B (Correcting Sentence Fragments)
39. B (Using Possessives)
40. A (Combining Sentences)

Writing

Use the scoring rubric on page 19 and the criteria for narrative writing on page 20 to evaluate students' written responses.

Listening

41. B (Setting)
42. D (Sequence of Events)
43. A (Problem and Solution)
44. C (Plot)
45. A (Make Inferences)
46. B (Main Idea and Details)
47. C (Cause and Effect)
48. D (Compare and Contrast)
49. A (Cause and Effect)
50. C (Summarize)

rSkills Midyear Test (Level b) Answer Key

Sample Questions

Sample **A.** D

Sample **B.** B

Comprehension

1.	C	(Sequence of Events)
2.	A	(Setting)
3.	A	(Problem and Solution)
4.	D	(Character)
5.	B	(Plot)
6.	C	(Character)
7.	B	(Sequence of Events)
8.	D	(Main Idea and Details)
9.	C	(Sequence of Events)
10.	A	(Summarize)
11.	C	(Main Idea and Details)
12.	A	(Summarize)
13.	D	(Setting)
14.	B	(Sequence of Events)
15.	D	(Character)
16.	A	(Plot)
17.	C	(Main Idea and Details)
18.	D	(Main Idea and Details)
19.	C	(Problem and Solution)
20.	A	(Summarize)

Vocabulary/Word Study

21.	B	(Context Clues)
22.	B	(Compound Words)
23.	D	(Synonyms)
24.	C	(Antonyms)
25.	A	(Idioms)
26.	C	(Word Families)
27.	B	(Suffixes)
28.	A	(Prefixes)

Vocabulary/Word Study *(continued)*

29.	C	(Homophones)
30.	D	(Homophones)

Grammar, Usage, and Mechanics

31.	C	(Using Correct Word Order)
32.	A	(Correcting Sentence Fragments)
33.	B	(Using Irregular Verbs)
34.	C	(Using End Punctuation)
35.	D	(Using Compound Sentences)
36.	B	(Using Commas in a Series)
37.	D	(Using Correct Verb Tenses)
38.	A	(Combining Sentences)
39.	C	(Using Capitals)
40.	A	(Correcting Run-on Sentences)

Writing

Use the scoring rubric on page 19 and the criteria for expository writing on page 20 to evaluate students' written responses.

Listening

41.	C	(Sequence of Events)
42.	A	(Problem and Solution)
43.	B	(Setting)
44.	D	(Character)
45.	B	(Plot)
46.	B	(Main Idea and Details)
47.	A	(Sequence of Events)
48.	C	(Problem and Solution)
49.	A	(Main Idea and Details)
50.	D	(Summarize)

rSkills End-of-Year Test (Level b) Answer Key

Sample Questions

Sample **A.** A

Sample **B.** C

Comprehension

1. B (Plot)
2. D (Compare and Contrast)
3. A (Character)
4. D (Theme)
5. B (Cause and Effect)
6. A (Cause and Effect)
7. C (Make Inferences)
8. D (Main Idea and Details)
9. B (Setting)
10. B (Plot)
11. D (Problem and Solution)
12. C (Sequence of Events)
13. A (Character)
14. C (Make Inferences)
15. B (Compare and Contrast)
16. D (Cause and Effect)
17. D (Problem and Solution)
18. A (Problem and Solution)
19. C (Summarize)
20. B (Summarize)

Vocabulary/Word Study

21. C (Multiple-Meaning Words)
22. A (Noun Endings)
23. A (Synonyms)
24. B (Suffixes)
25. C (Antonyms)
26. B (Latin and Greek Roots)
27. C (Homophones)
28. D (Word Families)

Vocabulary/Word Study *(continued)*

29. C (Using a Dictionary)
30. D (Verb Endings)

Grammar, Usage, and Mechanics

31. B (Correcting Sentence Fragments)
32. B (Avoiding Double Negatives)
33. C (Using Adverbs)
34. A (Using Quotation Marks)
35. D (Combining Sentences)
36. A (Using Subject and Object Pronouns)
37. D (Identifying Sentences and Fragments)
38. A (Using Adjectives That Compare)
39. D (Using Possessives)
40. B (Using Conjunctions)

Writing

Use the scoring rubric on page 19 and the criteria for narrative writing on page 20 to evaluate students' written responses.

Listening

41. B (Sequence of Events)
42. A (Setting)
43. C (Problem and Solution)
44. D (Plot)
45. A (Make Inferences)
46. C (Main Idea and Details)
47. A (Cause and Effect)
48. A (Compare and Contrast)
49. D (Cause and Effect)
50. D (Summarize)

Overview of Tested Skills

Strand/Skill	Below Grade-Level Tests							Grade-Level Tests						
	1a	2a	3a	4a	5a	Mid	End	1b	2b	3b	4b	5b	Mid	End
Comprehension														
Main Idea and Details	✓	✓				✓	✓	✓	✓				✓	✓
Sequence of Events	✓	✓				✓	✓	✓	✓				✓	✓
Character		✓	✓			✓	✓		✓	✓		✓	✓	✓
Setting		✓	✓		✓	✓	✓		✓	✓		✓	✓	✓
Plot		✓	✓		✓	✓	✓		✓	✓		✓	✓	✓
Theme			✓			✓	✓							✓
Summarize		✓	✓	✓		✓	✓		✓	✓	✓		✓	✓
Problem and Solution			✓	✓		✓	✓			✓	✓		✓	✓
Cause and Effect				✓	✓	✓	✓				✓	✓		✓
Compare and Contrast				✓	✓	✓	✓				✓	✓		✓
Make Inferences					✓	✓	✓					✓		✓
Vocabulary/Word Study														
Prefixes	✓					✓	✓	✓					✓	✓
Suffixes	✓			✓		✓	✓	✓			✓		✓	✓
Synonyms	✓			✓		✓	✓	✓			✓		✓	✓
Antonyms	✓				✓	✓	✓	✓				✓	✓	✓
Word Families		✓	✓			✓	✓		✓	✓			✓	✓
Noun Endings					✓	✓	✓					✓		✓
Homophones		✓	✓			✓	✓		✓	✓			✓	✓
Compound Words		✓				✓	✓		✓				✓	✓
Using a Dictionary				✓	✓	✓	✓				✓	✓		✓
Multiple-Meaning Words			✓	✓		✓	✓			✓	✓		✓	✓
Idioms			✓			✓	✓			✓			✓	✓
Context Clues		✓				✓	✓		✓				✓	✓
Verb Endings				✓			✓				✓		✓	
Latin or Greek Roots							✓							✓

Overview of Tested Skills 301

Overview of Tested Skills (continued)

Strand/Skill	Below Grade-Level Tests							Grade-Level Tests						
	1a	2a	3a	4a	5a	Mid	End	1b	2b	3b	4b	5b	Mid	End
Grammar, Usage, and Mechanics														
Identifying Sentences and Fragments	✓				✓	✓	✓	✓				✓		✓
Correcting Sentence Fragments	✓				✓	✓	✓	✓				✓	✓	✓
Correcting Run-On Sentences		✓				✓			✓				✓	
Using Correct Verb Tense		✓				✓			✓				✓	
Using Irregular Verbs			✓			✓				✓			✓	
Subject-Verb Agreement			✓							✓				
Using Subject and Object Pronouns				✓			✓				✓			✓
Using Adjectives That Compare				✓			✓				✓			✓
Using Adverbs					✓		✓					✓		✓
Using End Punctuation								✓					✓	
Using Capitals								✓					✓	
Using Correct Word Order	✓	✓				✓			✓				✓	
Using Commas in a Series	✓	✓							✓					
Using Commas With Introductory Words			✓			✓				✓				
Using Possessives			✓			✓				✓				
Avoiding Double Negatives				✓			✓				✓			✓
Using Quotation Marks				✓			✓				✓			✓
Identifying Simple and Compound Sentences	✓				✓		✓	✓				✓		✓
Combining Sentences		✓			✓	✓	✓		✓			✓	✓	✓
Using Conjunctions			✓			✓	✓			✓				✓
Using Compound Sentences				✓		✓					✓		✓	

Overview of Tested Skills *(continued)*

Strand/Skill	Below Grade-Level Tests							Grade-Level Tests						
	1a	2a	3a	4a	5a	Mid	End	1b	2b	3b	4b	5b	Mid	End
Writing														
Expository	✓							✓						
Response to Literature		✓				✓			✓				✓	
Persuasive			✓							✓				
Descriptive				✓							✓			
Narrative					✓		✓					✓		✓
Listening														
Main Idea and Details						✓	✓						✓	✓
Sequence of Events						✓	✓						✓	✓
Character						✓							✓	
Setting						✓	✓						✓	✓
Plot						✓	✓						✓	✓
Summarize						✓	✓						✓	✓
Problem and Solution						✓	✓						✓	✓
Cause and Effect							✓						✓	✓
Compare and Contrast							✓						✓	✓
Make Inferences							✓						✓	✓